Churchill and the Great Republic

Churchill and the Great Republic

Preface by Mary Churchill Soames

Foreword by James H. Billington,
THE LIBRARIAN OF CONGRESS

Essays by Martin Gilbert,
Allen Packwood, and Daun van Ee

[signature] Allen Packwood
23/05/06
(English style !)

The Library of Congress, Washington, D.C.

in association with

D Giles Limited, London

The exhibition *Churchill and the Great Republic*
and its programming were made possible by the generous
support of John W. Kluge and the Annenberg Foundation.

The accompanying publication and symposia were produced
in association with and through the support of
The Churchill Centre, Washington, D.C.

BACK COVER:
President Harry S. Truman's autograph letter to Winston S. Churchill, July 10, 1948,
Churchill Archives Centre, Churchill Papers, CHUR 2/158/43

FRONT COVER:
Franklin D. Roosevelt and Winston S. Churchill meet aboard the U.S.S. *Augusta*, Placentia Bay,
Newfoundland, August 9, 1941, Library of Congress, Washington, DC, Manuscript Division

FRONTISPIECE:
Photograph of a painting of young Winston S. Churchill during the Boer War (1899-1902),
Library of Congress, Washington DC, Prints and Photograph Division
Frontispiece used by permission of Associated Press

TABLE OF CONTENTS

Preface

Mary Churchill Soames   6

Foreword

James H. Billington, The Librarian of Congress   8

Introduction
Martin Gilbert   10

From Buffalo Bill to the Atomic Bomb:
Impressions of America from the Churchill Papers
Allen Packwood   13

'Incandescent Quality':
Churchill Materials in the Library of Congress
Daun van Ee   57

About the Library of Congress   91

About The Churchill Centre   92

About the Churchill Archives Centre   94

I feel greatly honored to have been asked to write the preface to the book that celebrates this important exhibition—"Churchill and the Great Republic"—to be held in the supremely prestigious location of the Library of Congress.

Months of thought and preparation on the part of many people on both sides of the Atlantic have gone into the realization of this exhibition, demonstrating a close and fruitful collaboration between the Library of Congress in Washington, D.C., and the Churchill Archives Centre in Cambridge, U.K., with the further support of The Churchill Centre in Washington. This collaboration embodies the working ties between the "English-Speaking Peoples" that my father so passionately believed in, and for which he strived unremittingly in his lifetime.

A mass of written material survives that bears witness to Winston Churchill's lifelong links with the United States. These writings largely chronicle his North American visits, beginning with his first in November 1895, just short of his twenty-first birthday, to his last visit over half a century later in 1961 when he was in his eighty-seventh year. A mass of relevant material, which the exhibit presents, is to be found in the voluminous holdings of his kinsman and close friend "Sunny," the ninth Duke of Marlborough, and also later in his career, in the papers of his great wartime colleague and friend, Averell Harriman.

The Churchill Papers, one component of this exhibit, comprise some two and a half thousand boxes, which contain papers relating to every part of his long life: political correspondence and official papers, drafts of his speeches and proofs of his books (corrected in his own hand), and letters recording minutiae from some of his diverse interests outside the life of politics and writing. For example, the Churchill Papers even contain detailed instructions to the gardeners about the care and management of his precious black swans at Chartwell. There are letters from friends and family members (I am touched to find lurking there my earliest childhood letters to him). But most valuable and revealing—a veritable treasure trove— is the collection of letters between Winston and his beloved wife Clementine, written over the more than fifty years of their relationship: no serious student of Churchill can afford to overlook these.

Many of the letters and papers deal with his visits to America, both in peacetime and war: notes for his famous speeches and broadcasts, and his official communications with Roosevelt and subsequent U.S. presidents. This splendid exhibition will appeal to many different people—and to various age groups. The majority of those who visit the exhibition will not remember World War II— although their grandparents and parents certainly may—nor will recall the cause for which that generation on both sides of the Atlantic worked and fought—and many died. But the compelling interest and appeal of what can be seen here lies in the extraordinary fact that history spanning 150 years or more, can be traced in the life and works of one man—Winston Churchill—who was the child of both America and Britain.

The whole vast corpus of the Churchill Papers, which is held by the Sir Winston Churchill Archive Trust, is housed and in the care of the Churchill Archives Centre, at Churchill College, Cambridge, England. The Centre itself was first built thanks to the vision and princely generosity of a number of former United States ambassadors to the Court of St. James, and other distinguished American citizens—further marking the strong ties between Winston Churchill and the United States, of which he himself was an Honorary Citizen.

As I learned to understand from my childhood onward, my father deeply cherished the blood link with America he possessed through his famously beautiful Yankee mother, Jennie Jerome, of whom he always spoke with so much love and admiration. And I know how his spirits lifted, even in the darkest days, whenever a transatlantic visit—however fraught with the dangers and discomforts of wartime journeys—was in view. His feelings echoed the lines quoted by him in a broadcast in April 1941: "But westward, look the land is bright!"

Mary Churchill Soames

In 2004, the Library of Congress joins with the Churchill Archives Centre, a division of Churchill College, Cambridge University, to present an exhibition on Winston Spencer Churchill's long and consequential relationship with the United States of America: "Churchill and the Great Republic." The title, taken from his own words, reflects Churchill's admiration for the land, people, and institutions of the country that was the birthplace of his mother, Brooklyn-born Jennie Jerome. Many of the materials for the exhibit are drawn from the unparalleled collection of Churchill materials in the Churchill Archives, exhibited comprehensively in the United States for the first time. Even more items come from the rich, multi-format sources of the Library of Congress; some of these, newly uncovered, are similarly shown for the first time. The Library of Congress, in association with The Churchill Centre in Washington, D.C., will mark the occasion by conducting two symposia at the Library. The Churchill Centre in Washington, D.C., also helped initiate and has supported this publication, which presents a sampling of the fascinating objects displayed at the exhibit, together with brief essays to put them into context. An electronic version of this exhibit, accessible through the Library of Congress website at http://www.loc.gov, will make the information and images even more widely available.

This exhibition takes place at an especially appropriate time. The year 2004 marks the sixtieth anniversary of the Allied invasion of Nazi-occupied France—D-Day—which for the United States was the pivotal event of World War II. During that titanic struggle Winston Churchill earned a lasting place in the hearts of the American people. The example he set, as prime minister of the United Kingdom, continues to inspire America and the world. His courage, determination, and rhetorical eloquence instantly came to mind after the terrorist attacks of September 11, 2001. Those who sought to cope with that crisis tried to emulate his legendary wartime leadership, and undoubtedly future statesmen will continue to look back to Churchill as they face the challenges of an often dangerous and uncertain world.

James H. Billington
The Librarian of Congress

INTRODUCTION

I feel privileged to write an introduction to this Library of Congress publication, compiled by two masters of the archivist's art, Allen Packwood, head of the Churchill Archives Centre, Churchill College, Cambridge, and Daun van Ee, manuscript specialist at the Library of Congress and curator of this exhibition. The exhibition gains great strength from the many letters it displays written by Churchill himself at different periods of his long and full life.

Churchill was a prolific writer. His childhood letters attest to his ability to wield a pen from his earliest years, and to convey strong sentiments, fun and affection. His letters from the battlefield—one, reprinted here, written in pencil —are vivid and honest portrayals of war. He could confide his innermost political thoughts, and his most tender sentiments of affection, in pen and ink. His first books, substantial tomes, were written out by him in longhand. His early political speeches were almost all written out by hand, with copious corrections made as he rehearsed and honed what he wanted to say.

In the first decade of the twentieth century, with the arrival of his first full-time secretary, Miss Anning, Churchill began to dictate his speeches, word for word and phrase for phrase. They were always his own work: "My best endeavour," he called them. His secretaries knew how to type out his speeches from dictation into what they called "Psalm form," an almost poetic version, which he would amend and polish, and from which he would read.

Churchill took enormous trouble to polish and perfect his speeches, not so much for rhetorical flourishes—although these could, from his earliest years, be magnificent— but to set out an argument in careful and persuasive stages, to lead his listener step by step through a controversial or complex topic. In Parliament, he could speak for well over an hour in careful, cautious, conciliatory tones, as he led a reluctant or even hostile House of Commons towards the point of view or piece of legislation he wished to see accepted.

On entering government in 1905, Churchill drafted, partly in his own hand, a substantial body of legislation that he then introduced to Parliament to enhance the well-being of the British people, including those trapped by poverty, employed in harsh conditions, or incarcerated in prison, for all of whose rights he fought. Among his legislative achievements was the introduction of a statutory tea break for all those working in shops and factories.

In 1915, when Churchill was in a political wilderness as a result of the intrigue of his Conservative Party opponents, he wrote to his brother Jack: "God for a month of power—and a good shorthand writer." Power was not to be his, in the form he was convinced he could use most effectively, for another twenty-five years. But good shorthand writers were to be his in abundance, enabling him to give birth to magisterial books, State Papers, ministerial memoranda, diplomatic, political, and military telegrams—including more than a thousand wartime messages to President Roosevelt—many hundreds of newspaper and magazine articles, tens of thousands of letters, and even a substantial film script.

These shorthand writers, the conduit for so many Churchill documents, included Harry Beckenham, who was with him in 1915 and again when he returned to government office in 1917, staying at his side and taking down his thoughts and dictation until 1922. Beckenham was succeeded by Lettice Fisher, who was with Churchill when he was Chancellor of the Exchequer, presenting five consecutive national budgets, and introducing, among other reform measures, state-aided pensions for widows and orphans. He also abolished the tax on tea, which had been imposed on the British public in the reign of Queen Elizabeth I—and had been the spark that had ignited the American Revolution.

Churchill's prolific writing capacity was sustained from 1936 by his appointment of Kathleen Hill as his first resident secretary. She, and a dozen other secretaries who joined the team at different times were the silent, unsung heroes of Churchill's literary productivity. For the last three years of World War II, Elizabeth Layton and Marion Spicer were at his side, even amid the gunfire of Athens on Christmas Day.

In the course of my work in the Churchill vineyard, culminating in my one-volume biography *Churchill, A Life*, I learned to recognize the handiwork of the typists—Churchill's "young ladies"—his dependence on their skills and devotion, and his appreciation of their efforts.

The Library of Congress exhibition vividly displays Churchill's love of the written word, and writing zeal. The archives of Churchill College, Cambridge, reveal myriad facts of his multifaceted life, career, and personality. His letters to his mother mark an intimacy, and an independence, rare in the relationship of mother and son in the political firmament. His demands to his mother were persistent, but despite her frequent caveats at his impatience or impetuousness she nearly always hastened to fulfill them. It was she who, when he was a young soldier in distant India, responded to his call for books—and yet more books—with which he could educate himself. His letters to his brother show the impact of the United States of America during his first visit in 1895. The remarkable letters to his cousin, the ninth Duke of Marlborough—one of the treasures of the Library of Congress—show how confiding he could be of his innermost thoughts, fears, and hopes.

That ability to express his inner thoughts is also evident in each of Churchill's letters to his wife Clementine (which his son Randolph, and then myself, published in full in the respective volumes of the Churchill biography). At the age of eighty-eight Churchill was still writing in his own hand to his wife of fifty-five years: "My darling one," he wrote then—his handwriting impaired but not broken by a series of strokes—"this is only to give you my fondest love and kisses a hundred times repeated." He underlined the words "a hundred times repeated" and went on: "I am a pretty dull and paltry scribbler; but my stick as it writes carries my heart along with it."

This exhibition, covering the long and crowded span of Churchill's personal and political life, opens a window into the world of that "paltry scribbler," who loved language, used it in triumph and adversity to make his points and fight his battles, and who was confident that, by writing and debate, liberty could be preserved, democracy sustained, and the well-being of mankind enhanced.

Sir Martin Gilbert

Churchill and the Great Republic

From Buffalo Bill to the Atomic Bomb:
Impressions of America from the Churchill Papers

From Buffalo Bill to the Atomic Bomb:
Impressions of America from the Churchill Papers

Brighton, Buffalo Bill, and the "Boneless Wonder"

It is perhaps fitting that one of the earliest references by Winston Churchill to an American was to another historical icon: the famous adventurer and showman William F. Cody, known as "Buffalo Bill."

This reference to "Buffalow Bill [sic]" occurs in a letter written from school to his mother. The letter is the culmination of one of Churchill's earliest concerted campaigns: a campaign to persuade Lady Randolph Churchill to allow him to leave his seat of learning in Brighton and attend Queen Victoria's Golden Jubilee celebrations in London. Although marked simply "Sunday," the letter must date from Sunday June 12, 1887, and follows on earlier letters dated May 24 and 31, and postmarked June 11, all of which refer to the Jubilee celebrations and Winston's desire to be present.

Churchill was just twelve years old. He was being educated at a private school in Brunswick Road, Hove, just outside the popular seaside resort of Brighton, on the English south coast. The school was run by two elderly sisters named Thomson, and it is to one of these that Churchill urges his mother to write, even going so far as to spell out the form of words he thinks she should use. His template for her letter ends in her initials, "J.S.C.," for Jennie Spencer-Churchill. The letter certainly reveals the ingenuity, determination, and strength of character inherent in the young schoolboy, while the drawings reveal an early artistic bent and clearly capture his enthusiasm for his subject.

The letter refers to some of the most important people in Winston's childhood: his mother, Lady Randolph Churchill; his brother, John, called "Jack"; and his nanny, Mrs. Everest. It is written to his mother, and was kept by her among her papers. Lady Randolph Churchill was an American by birth; christened Jennie, she was the eldest daughter of the businessman Leonard Jerome. She had married the British politician Lord Randolph Churchill, second son of the Duke of Marlborough, in April 1874, after a lightning romance. Winston arrived quickly thereafter, the following November, to be followed four years later by his brother, Jack. A great beauty and society figure, Lady Randolph was a dominating if distant presence in Winston's childhood. In his own account of his early life, he compares her to a "fairy princess" and the Evening Star, and admits, "I loved her dearly—but at a distance." It was Mrs. Everest, whom Winston nicknamed and wrote to as "Womany" or "Woom," who provided the commonplace affection and practical support.

It appears that this letter won the day and secured Winston his place at the Jubilee, the first of the many royal occasions, coronations, and funerals that would occur during a life that encompassed the reigns of six monarchs, from Queen Victoria to Queen Elizabeth II. The Jubilee festivities centered around the Service of Thanksgiving at Westminster Abbey on June 21, at which Lady Randolph was certainly present. We know from a further letter to his mother that Winston was detained in Brighton until almost the last moment. He certainly did not return on the eighteenth as he had hoped, and was still in Brighton on the nineteenth, from where he wrote in desperation, complaining that he was "nearly mad with suspense" and begging Lady Randolph to "write before it is too late." Then on June 24 he wrote to say that he was back at school, expressing the hope that she would soon forget his bad behavior while at home. It seems that he got his wish and made the most of his opportunity!

Winston would not have been allowed to accompany his mother into Westminster Abbey, but that was not what he wanted to see. Like most schoolboys he was interested in the accompanying parades and public entertainment, and more particularly in seeing "Buffalow Bill" and his Wild West show. According to one author, it was during the Jubilee festivities that Winston was taken by his Uncle John [Leslie] to the circus to see the strong man and a celebrated freak show act called "The Boneless Wonder." If so, it is not clear whether young Churchill was actually allowed to see the act. Years later, speaking in the House of Commons in 1931, he made the following com-

Winston S. Churchill's autograph letter to his mother from his school in Brighton, June 12, 1887, Churchill Archives Centre, Churchill Papers, CHAR 28/14/18

ment while verbally attacking the Labour leader and then British prime minister Ramsay MacDonald :

> I remember when I was a child being taken to the celebrated Barnum's circus, which contained an exhibition of freaks and monstrosities, but the exhibit on the programme which I desired to see was the one described as 'The Boneless Wonder'. My parents judged that spectacle would be too revolting and demoralising for my youthful eyes, and I have waited fifty years to see 'The Boneless Wonder' sitting on the Treasury Bench.

[Transcript of Letter from Winston S. Churchill to Lady Randolph Churchill, June 12, 1887]

	29–30	Brunswick Road
[12 June 1887]*		Brighton
		Sunday

My dear mamma,

    I hope you are as well as I am. I am writing this letter to back up my last. I hope you will not disappoint me. I can think of nothing else but Jubilee. Uncertainty is at all times perplexing write to me by return post please!!! I love you so much dear mummy and I know you love me too much to disappoint me. Do write to tell me what you intend to do. I must come home, I feel I must. Write to miss Thomson a letter after this principle so: - "my dear _____

    Could you allow Winston to come up to London, on Saturday the 18th for the Jubilee. I should like him to see the procession very much, and I also promised him that he should come up for the Jubilee

    I remain

    Yours

    J.S.C. "

I think that the above will hit its mark, anyhow you can try. I know you will be successfull [sic].

    I am looking forward to seeing Buffalow Bill, yourself, Jack, Everest, and <u>home</u>.

I would sooner come home for the Jubilee and have no amusement at all than stay down here and have tremendous fun. The weather is fine.

Please, as you love me, do as I have begged you.

Love to all

I remain as ever

your loving son

Winny

For Heavens sake Remember!!!

First Impressions of the United States

Major James B. Pond, self-styled "proprietor and manager," was the New York agent charged with arranging Churchill's first North American lecture tour. Here he writes to Churchill's mother, the widowed Lady Randolph Churchill. She had recently become Mrs. George Cornwallis West, having somewhat controversially taken as her second husband a young army captain, a man only a few days older than Winston himself.

The letter proves that by November 1900 Winston Churchill was already a celebrity. Major Pond begins by congratulating the mother on the success of her son, "a man who has attained a success at twenty-six which most men would count brilliant at fifty." In fact, Winston Churchill was only twenty-five when this letter was written, celebrating his twenty-sixth birthday four weeks later, on November 30, 1900, just prior to his arrival in the United States. Pond seems to have got this incorrect information from an article in the *New York Herald*, which he encloses as illustration of the media interest in Churchill's impending arrival. Winston had already seen military action in Cuba, India, and the Sudan. He had published numerous newspaper articles and three books about his experiences, and even found time to write a novel. Yet it was his escape from Boer captivity in South Africa and his subsequent election to the British Parliament that had elevated him onto the international stage.

This was not his first transatlantic voyage, nor his first visit to New York. Just five years before, in November 1895, he had stopped in New York en route to Cuba, where he had spent his twenty-first birthday as an observer attached to a Spanish column skirmishing with Cuban guerrillas. Then his visit had lasted just over a week, and had been very much a tourist trip, with an outing to a courthouse, a tour of West Point, and many society dinners and receptions. He recorded his first impressions of his mother's birthplace in letters back to his family, including the observation to his brother, Jack, that, "the essence of American journalism is vulgarity divested of truth."

By 1900, Churchill's focus was on work, not leisure or adventure. The catalyst for his second journey to New York was the desire for money. Churchill was keen to capitalize on his newfound fame and status, unsure of how long it might last, and to earn some money with which to underwrite his new and expensive political career. A two-month lecture tour was planned, taking in New York and Washington, D.C., with venues as far west as St. Louis and St. Paul, and incorporating Montreal, Toronto, Ottawa, and other centers in eastern Canada. The title of his lecture series was "The War in South Africa as I saw it."

Major James B. Pond was the man hired to put together Churchill's program. His own stationery, which survives on a later letter to Churchill, advertised his ability to arrange "lectures, concerts and all descriptions of musical, lyceum and literary entertainments." It also boasted a whole series of names of lecturers, specialty acts, lecture reading, readers, combinations, and soloists for the season of 1900–1901. These included Sir Robert Ball, the University of Cambridge astronomer; Samuel L. Clemens, better known as Mark Twain, "if he lectures"; and Joseph Howard, Jr., with his illustrated talk, "New York as She Now Is."

The Pond letter and attached cutting make it clear that the new Mrs. Cornwallis West, or Lady Randolph Churchill-West as some of the American press styled her, was at least as well known in East Coast circles as her famous son. Her connections and influence over powerful men had already helped open doors for her elder son, and Major Pond was under no illusion that she would help double his audiences. Perhaps unfortunately, given Churchill's subsequent complaints about numbers attending his lectures, Mrs. Cornwallis West chose to stay at home.

Churchill arrived in New York on December 8, having traveled across the Atlantic on the Cunard liner *Lucania*. Some of the contemporary papers reported that the VIP reception committee, rumored to include such worthies as Vice President-elect Theodore Roosevelt, the governor-elect, and the mayor, had failed to materialize. It is clear that Churchill's American cousin, Mrs. Jordan L. Mott, Jr., was present, along with a group of friends. If Churchill was disappointed at the pier side, it seems likely that this disappointment would have evaporated as he emerged from the port to be met by Major Pond and the press corps. Whatever his private views on their "vulgarity," Churchill quickly found himself answering reporters' questions on the brutality of British policy in South Africa and on the character of the army commander Lord Kitchener. He also had to deny rumors that he had come to the United States to find a wealthy bride!

It is clear from the newspaper reports that Churchill was walking into a minefield. British policy in South Africa was not popular in the United States, and he was required to walk a fine line, defending his country's conduct of the war while praising the fighting skills of the Boer. Pro-Boer and anti-British sentiment may well have contributed to the somewhat poorer-than-expected attendance at the subsequent lectures. Churchill wrote to his mother from the Hotel Touraine in Boston on December 21, 1900, explaining, "I got on very well with the audiences over here, although on several occasions I have had almost one-half of them strongly pro-Boer, and of course I do not have the great crowds that always came in England." However, it is clear from the same letter that he also blamed Major Pond for exaggerating the level of interest. As the tour went on, his spirits seemed to sink, and by New Year's Day 1901 he was writing to her again from Toronto describing his falling out with Pond, whom he now labeled "a vulgar Yankee impresario."

Major James B. Pond's letter to Winston S. Churchill's mother, November 2, 1900, Churchill Archives Centre, Churchill Papers, CHAR 28/66/80-81

NEW YORK, **Nov. 2nd,** 1900

Mrs. Cornwallis West,
135a Great Cumberland Place,

London, W.

My Dear Madam:-

I want to congratulate you on the success of your
son,- a man who has attained a success at twenty-six which
most men would count brilliant at fifty.

Have you any idea how green your memory is here
in New York City ? I would suggest that you accompany your
son on the voyage and witness his reception here. It
seems to me it would be a very proud day for you, and your
friends here would appreciate it, and I need not add that it
would doubly enhance the value of the lecture.

Yours Very Truly,

J. B. Pond

The tour may not have brought the financial rewards that Churchill wanted, but neither was it a complete disaster. It established his name in East Coast literary circles, and saw him introduced to many of the great and good. In Washington he met President McKinley. In Albany he finally met and dined with Theodore Roosevelt, and in New York he was introduced to Mark Twain. By the time he set sail for home at the beginning of February, he had traveled extensively in the eastern part of America and broadened his knowledge of and contacts in the New World. He sailed back to a Britain in mourning for the death of Queen Victoria, and to the beginning of his own political career. It would be twenty-eight years before he returned, and during this period he would rise to hold some of the highest—although not yet the highest—offices of the British state.

[Transcript of Letter from Major James B. Pond to Mrs. Cornwallis West, November 2, 1900]

[Photograph of Winston S. Churchill]
Winston Spencer Churchill's American Tour
1900–1901   New York, Nov. 2nd, 1900

conducted by
J.B. POND
Everett House 218 Fourth
Avenue NEW YORK

Mrs. Cornwallis West
35a Great Cumberland Place,
London, W.

My Dear Madam:-

I want to congratulate you on the success of your son,—a man who has attained a success at twenty-six which most men would count brilliant at fifty.

Have you any idea how green your memory is here in New York City? I would suggest that you accompany your son on the voyage and witness his reception here. It seems to me it would be a very proud day for you, and your friends here would appreciate it, and I need not add that it would doubly enhance the value of the lecture.

Yours Very Truly
J. B. Pond

WINSTON SPENCER CHURCHILL
What Julian Ralph writes from
London to the New York Herald

The people of America are awaiting the coming of Mr. Winston Churchill, who is to lecture on the Transvaal war in all the great cities over there.

They know as much about the historic Churchill family as do the English themselves. They remember his beautiful mother as one of the first Americans to marry into England's nobility, and they will be pleased to hear that he is proud to acknowledge himself "half an American." They have read his newspaper letters and his books; they expect him to have a great future, and they wonder what sort of man he is.

Winston Leonard Spencer Churchill is twenty-six years old, with the mind of a far older man and the vitality and enthusiasm of a far younger one. He is a well-built man, about the average height, with very broad shoulders and the strong frame of his mother's people. But you have to forget and look away from his face in order to see his frame, for his face is of a highly nervous, wholly intellectual type.

He has all the nervous energy and fire that wore out and burned up his father's brilliant life. But he has also, as I have said, the physique of his mother's people. Of his father there is nothing apparent or repeated in his flesh except Lord Randolph's brow. But in temperament, originality, dash, eloquence, and the magic art of swaying men he is his father's promissory note, payable when he is more mature.

West Coast Adventures

Churchill's most extensive tour of the United States arose from a political defeat. The British general election of May 1929 had seen the election of Ramsay MacDonald and the first Labour government. Churchill had been chancellor of the exchequer, the secretary of state for the treasury, in Stanley Baldwin's Conservative government since the end of 1924. Before that he had served as minister in Asquith's Liberal government from 1908 to 1915, and in Lloyd George's national government from 1917 to 1922, enjoying almost two decades of high political office.

Lady Soames has described her father's three-month North American tour as "part holiday and part of a programme of speeches and lectures in major cities." Churchill was good at combining pleasure with profit, and took with him his son, Randolph, his brother, Jack, and Jack's son, Johnnie. The party crossed the Atlantic in some style on board the *Empress of Australia*, arriving in Quebec on August 10. From here they made their way across Canada, leaving Victoria for Seattle and the United States on Friday, September 6.

Clementine Churchill was recovering from the removal of her tonsils, and so had been unable to come on the North American trip. Winston kept her informed of the party's progress in a series of letters and bulletins, some handwritten, some typescript, which were kept by Clementine and survive among her personal correspondence. In the letter that appears to have been written in Los Angeles on about September 18, Churchill comments on his arrival in Seattle and his encounter with the local customs official. This was the era of prohibition. Churchill's special "diplomatic visas" enabled him to bring in alcohol for his personal use, but this did not prevent a thorough examination of the party's luggage. He may not have been amused at the time, but Churchill could not resist telling his wife what happened next, how the customs official drove the whole party to the local hotel, where they were all entertained with iced beer, the customs official explaining that "the United States was not interested in the 'ultimate consumer.'"

This experience can only have strengthened Churchill's instinctive opposition to prohibition. On his return, he wrote up his observations on contemporary American society in a series of newspaper articles. He devoted one to prohibition, describing it as a "spectacle at once comic and pathetic," and expressing his conviction that "no folly is more costly than the folly of intolerant idealism." He also had a practical objection to the anti-alcohol legislation introduced by the Eighteenth Amendment, describing the results as the vastest game of "hunt the slipper that was ever known."

The letters to Clementine indicate that Churchill did not suffer unduly from these restrictions, sampling sacramental wine outside San Francisco, "every kind of liquor" at the Los Angeles Biltmore, and having his very own "Gannymede"—the cup bearer to the Greek gods—in the form of his son, Randolph, to furnish a private supply.

This was Churchill's only visit to the American West Coast. If he was unimpressed by prohibition, he was most certainly impressed by the scenery and society through which he was now traveling. In his letters to Clementine, and at greater length in a subsequent article entitled "California," he enthuses about the giant redwood forests, the general standard of living, the San Francisco Bay Bridge, and the "carnival in fairyland" that is Los Angeles. He also describes a visit to the Lick Observatory, where he looked through a telescope at the rings of Saturn.

These positive impressions can only have been reinforced by the quality of the hospitality the Churchill party experienced. This is the theme of Churchill's letter to Clementine of September 29, in which he gives his impressions of the California elite. He was certainly exposed to a cross section of high society, mingling with both the Hollywood set and the local business community. The newspaper magnate William Randolph Hearst offered lavish hospitality, ably assisted by his two "wives," the "official" Mrs. Hearst, who presided at Hearst's mansion at San Simeon, and Marion Davies, the famous actress and Hearst's mistress, who acted as the hostess in Los Angeles. The doors of Hollywood were open to the British party and Churchill, a film lover, was clearly interested to meet a fellow countryman, the movie star Charlie Chaplin, whom he describes as "bolshy in politics & delightful in conversation." Chaplin's left-wing views would cause him trouble later in his career, but this letter captures him and Hollywood at a pivotal moment, wrestling with the transition from the silent movie to the era of the "talkies."

There is no doubt that Churchill was enjoying his trip, and catching a "swordfish" must have seemed the icing on the cake. In fact it was "168 pound stripped marlin caught in 24 minutes on regulation tuna club tackle...he [Churchill] was a guest of Ben Meyer and fished aboard Monty Foster's 'Sunbeam II'"—this according to information recently presented to the Churchill Archives Centre in Cambridge, England, by the Tuna Club of Los Angeles, along with a framed photograph of the proud fisherman and his catch.

Further hospitality was provided courtesy of Mr. Schwab, the president of Bethlehem Steel, who put his luxury railway car at Churchill's disposal. Later on this tour Churchill would visit the Bethlehem steel works with their mass-production techniques. He was seeing at first hand the wealth and potential of America, and could contrast the living standards and industrial practices with 1920's Britain.

This wealth was temporarily threatened by the Wall Street crash of October 1929. Churchill clearly did not see this coming. The letter suggests that he was so caught up in the glamour and riches of California that he was prepared to invest a further £3,000 of his own money in the stock market. His timing could not have been worse. The collapse in the value of shares hit his personal finances. He was in New York to watch it happen, creating a somewhat depressing end to his grand tour. Deprived of his ministerial salary and now his savings, he would be forced to rely on his writings and oratory to sustain his expensive lifestyle, with its many family, literary, and secretarial commitments.

[Transcript of Typescript Letter from Winston S. Churchill to Clementine Churchill, September 18, 1929]

? 1929*   *18th Los Angeles*

We left Victoria in state on Friday and entered the United States at Seattle. Some officials met us, including the head of the Customs, and in spite of diplomatic visas and other credentials he asked a lot of questions, to which we gave appropriate answers to the effect that we had no liquor <u>to declare.</u> He then drove us to the hotel, where the local hotel proprietor entertained the whole party with delicious iced beer. *The Customs gent explained that the United States was not interested "in the ultimate consumer"! O.K.*

We caught the night train, travelling on this occasion like the ordinary public but quite comfortably and at 5 o'clock on Saturday got out at Grants Pass. Here we were met by Mr. Gerald Campbell, the British Consul General at Chicago with his car, and oddly enough, by Morton Smart and his wife, who are on a holiday fishing here. We packed our light luggage into the motor car and set off on our six hundred mile journey. The greater part of it lay through the woods with these enormous trees. They are really astonishing. One we saw, the biggest, 380 foot high, three thousand or four thousand or even five thousand years old and it took fourteen of us to join our arms around its stem. The motoring was very long, at least ten hours a day and at first we were crowded. Half way, at Eureka, the Vice Consul, a young Oxford graduate, arrived in an open car in which I and Randolph travelled, so we were able to spread out.

We slept at two small country hotels, at Crescent City and Willit. Everything very simple, very clean, gushing water and hot baths, no servants and no liquor. However Randolph acts as an unfailing Gannymede. *Up to the present I have never been without what was necessary.*

(to be continued in my next bulletin)

[Text in italics is manuscript by Churchill]
* Year and question mark added by a later hand

[Transcript of Letter from Winston S. Churchill to Clementine Churchill, September 29, 1929]

La Cuesta Encantada*
[Engraving of Casa Del Monte]

Casa Del Monte*
San Simeon, Cal[ifornia]*

29 Sept. 1929?**
Barstow**

My darling Clemmie,

We are far from the enchanting scene depicted above. We are travelling across the Californian desert in Mr Schwab's car, & we have stopped for 2 hours at this oasis. We have left the train for a bath in the hotel, & as it is so nice & cool I will write you a few of the things it is wisest not to dictate

Hearst was most interesting to meet, & I got to like him—a grave simple child—with no doubt a nasty temper—playing with the most costly toys. A vast income always overspent: Ceaseless building & collecting not v[er]y discriminatingly works of art: two magnificent establishments, two charming wives; complete indifference to public opinion, a strong liberal & democratic outlook, a 15 million daily circulation, oriental hospitalities, extreme personal courtesy (to us at any rate) & the appearance of a Quaker elder—or perhaps better Mormon elder.

I told you about Mrs. H. (the official) & how agreeable she made herself. She is going to give us a dinner in N.Y. [New York] & look after the boys on their way through. At Los Angeles (hard g) we passed into the domain of Marion Davies; & were all charmed by her. she is not strikingly beautiful nor impressive in any way. But her personality is most attractive; naïve child like, <u>bon enfant</u>. She works all day at her films & returns to her palace on the ocean to bathe & entertain in the evenings. She asked us to use her house as if it was our own. But we tasted its comforts and luxuries only sparingly, dining two nights there after enormous dinner parties in our honour. We lunched frequently at her bungalow in the film works—a little Italian chapel sort of building v[er]y elegant where Hearst spends the day directing his newspapers on the telephone, & wrestling with his private Ch.[ancellor] of the Excheq[uer]—a harassed functionary who is constantly compelled to find money & threatens resignation daily.

We made g[rea]t friends with Charlie Chaplin. You c[oul]d not help liking him. The boys were fascinated by him. He is a marvellous comedian—bolshy in politics & delightful in conversation. He acted his new film for us in a wonderful way. It is to be his g[rea]t attempt to prove that the silent drama or pantomime is superior to the new talkies. Certainly if pathos & wit still count for anything it ought to win an easy victory.

I stayed in the main at the Biltmore hotel—wh[ich] is the last word in hotels. A Mr Page who obtained 'the honour' of entertaining us—a hearty Banker—refused to allow us to pay anything. the finest suite an excellent valet waiter—motor cars—& every kind of liquor—together with much self effacement, made these hospitalities agreeable. I met all the leading people & have heard on every side that my speech & talks (to circles of ten or twelve) have given much pleasure. I explained to them all about England & her affairs—showing how splendid & tolerant she was, & how we ought to work together. I gave a dinner & a lunch to the leading men I liked the best mostly British born, & all keenly pro-England, (with much difficulty I succeeded in extracting the cost of their meals from the Bill & paying them myself). There is a Mr Andrew Chaffey—President of the Californian Bank—to whom I took a g[rea]t liking. You w[oul]d have liked him v[er]y much. He is a Canadian-Australian-Californian. Immensely rich & respected—a sincere lover of our country, these Californian swells do not of course know Hearst. He dwells apart. The first time they had ever come into contact with him or the film world was at the luncheon he gave to me. They regard him as the Devil. But when they heard him speak in friendly terms about England, they all said how right I had been to stay with him & praised the good work.

Winston S. Churchill's letters to his wife, Clementine, September 18 & 29, 1929, Churchill Archives Centre, Baroness Spencer-Churchill Papers, CSCT 2/22/39 & 47

We left Victoria in state on Friday and entered the United
States at Seattle. Some officials met us, including the head of the
Customs, and in spite of diplomatic visas and other credentials
he asked a lot of questions, to which we gave appropriate answers
to the effect that we had no liquor to declare. He then drove us
to the hotel, where the local hotel proprietor entertained the
whole party with delicious iced beer. The Customs gent explained that
the United States was not interested "in the ultimate consumer"! O.K.
            We caught the night train, travelling on this ~~occasion~~
like the ordinary public but quite comfortably and at
Saturday got out at Grants Pass. Here we were met b
Campbell, the British Consul General at Chicago w
oddly enough, by Morton Smart and his wife, who a
fishing here. We packed our light luggage into
set off on our six hundred mile journey. The g
lay through the woods with these enormous tre
astonishing. One we saw, the biggest, 380 f
or four thousand or even five thousand year
of us to join our arms around its stem.
at least ten hours a day and at first we
              the
at Eureka,/Vice Consul, a young Oxford
car in which I and Randolph travelled

        We slept at two small coun
Willit. Everything very simple, ve
baths, no servants and no liquor.
untruthful Ganymede. Up
here without what was

        (to be c

CASA DEL MONTE   LA CUESTA ENCANTADA

SAN SIMEON, CAL.

My darling Clemmie,
                        We are far from the enchanting
scene depicted above. We are travelling across
the Californian desert in Mr. Schwab's car,
& we have stopped for 2 hours at this oasis
hotel, & as it is so nice & cool I will
write you a few of the things it is wiser
not to dictate

        Hearst was most interesting to meet,
& I got to like him — a grave simple
child — with no doubt a nasty temper —
playing with the most costly toys. A vast
income always overspent: Castles building
& collecting not very discriminating works of art:
two magnificent establishments, two charming

29 Sept. 1929
Barstow

There were four or five men here whom I thought v[er]y fine fellows indeed: & I believe they were equally pleased with my companionship.

We went on Sunday in a yacht to Catalina island 25 miles away. We had only one hour there. People go for weeks & months without catching a swordfish. So they all said it was quite useless my going out in the fishing boat wh[ich] had been provided. However I went out & of course I caught a monster in 20 minutes!

I have also made friends with Mr. Van Antwerp & his wife. He is a little old man—one of the heads of a far reaching stock-broking firm—a g[rea]t friend of England a reader of all my books – quite an old fashioned figure—

He is going to look after some of my money for me. His firm has the best information about the American market & I have opened an account with them in wh[ich] I have placed £3000. He will manipulate it with the best possible chances of success. All this looks v[er]y confiding—but I am sure it will prove wise.

Now I have to rush for my train wh[ich] is just off.

Goodbye my sweetest Clemmie

    With tender love

    from

    your devoted

    W.

                                * Printed

         ** Year and question mark added by later hand

A Close Encounter

On December 13, 1931, Winston Churchill stepped out of his taxicab into the path of an oncoming car. He had made the classic mistake of the Englishman in America and looked the wrong way. He was knocked down by a motor car on New York's Fifth Avenue.

Churchill was in the United States on another lecture tour, and had decided at short notice to spend the evening with his old friend Bernard Baruch. His bad luck began when he went out without Baruch's address. Unable to identify the apartment, he became increasingly impatient, and it was in a state of some frustration that he started to cross the road opposite Central Park to inquire at the most likely place.

The impact was sudden and violent. Churchill was left bleeding, shocked, and badly bruised, but no bones were broken. He was taken by ambulance to Lennox Hill Hospital for treatment, where he remained until December 21, before being released back into the care of his wife, Clementine, and daughter Diana, at the Waldorf Astoria Hotel. A receipt for $250 for "professional services rendered" during December 1931 by Dr. Foster Kennedy survives among his papers, along with many expressions of sympathy and good will.

That might have been the end of the matter. An unfortunate accident, a lecture tour cut short, and an early return to the United Kingdom. But that was not how Churchill reacted. From his convalescent bed he fired off several telegrams. On December 24 he contacted his friend and scientific adviser, Professor Frederick Lindemann, and asked him to calculate "what is impact or shock to stationary body two hundred pounds of motor car weighing two thousand four hundred pounds traveling [sic] thirty or thirtyfive miles per hour. Stop. This shock I took in my body being carried forward on the cowcatcher until brakes eventually stopped car when I dropped off." There is no mention of Christmas, and Churchill clearly had other things on his mind. He told Lindemann that he needed the figure for an article and that it must be "impressive."

Churchill wasted no time. On December 28 he cabled the Honorable Esmond Harmsworth, son of Lord Rothermere, owner of the British *Daily Mail* newspaper, to proudly inform him that he had now produced the finished article, some 3,600 words, and to ask about dates for the American release.

Lindemann's response arrived on December 30. It estimates the collision at some 6,000 pounds, the equivalent of falling thirty feet onto pavement, of stopping a brick dropped from 600 feet, or of absorbing two charges of buckshot point blank. The professor cannot resist teasing Churchill about the mitigating effect of the "thickness cushion surrounding skeleton" and congratulates him on "preparing [a] suitable cushion." It is an interesting corre-

Telegrams exchanged between Winston S. Churchill and Professor Lindemann, December 24 & 30, 1931, Churchill Archives Centre, Churchill Papers, CHAR 1/399B/151 & CHAR 1/222/20-21

spondence and gives an insight into the unlikely friendship between the aristocratic, extrovert British politician and the German-born, teetotal, vegetarian Oxford physicist. Churchill nicknamed Lindemann "Prof," and kept him as a member of his inner circle from the 1920's, giving him the ministerial position of paymaster general in both his 1940's wartime and 1950's peacetime governments, and rewarding him for his loyalty with an elevation to the peerage and the title of Lord Cherwell.

The *Daily Mail* published Churchill's account of his accident in two parts, on January 4 and 5, 1932. The first part was entitled "My New York Misadventure" and described the events up to impact. The second, entitled "I Was Conscious Through It All," described the aftermath and carried a photograph of the bandaged author in his wheelchair, with the caption "How it feels to be smashed up."

In the text Churchill admitted full liability for the accident. It was a wise and honorable move. The account was a great success, winning sympathy and widespread media interest. On March 9, 1932, he was interviewed for the radio by Mr. Hill of the Columbia Broadcasting System. Churchill began by describing his narrow escape: "It's not a jolly thing to be cut down by a motor car at 30 miles an hour. I think it would have knocked the life out of a great many people of my age. I was very lucky in the way it hit me." This prompted Mr. Hill to ask his guest if he believed in luck, to which Churchill answered: "I like to have it anyhow! Good luck and bad luck even out pretty well. What looks like bad luck may turn out to be good luck and vice versa. I've done a lot of foolish things that turned out well, and a lot of wise things that have turned out badly."

On this occasion there is no doubt that Churchill had ridden out his bad luck and turned it to his advantage. The episode reveals a lot about his physical and mental resilience, strengths he would need in abundance in the coming years. He was now fifty-seven years old, no longer held high political office, and appeared isolated from the leadership of the British Conservative Party over his opposition to greater Indian self-government. To many it seemed as if his career was over. This makes the next question in the CBS interview seem particularly poignant. Churchill was asked whether he believed that more "great troubles" were coming upon us, "for instance, another World War." His reply was emphatic: "I do not believe that we shall see another great war in our time."

[Transcript of Telegram from Winston S. Churchill to Professor Lindemann, December 24, 1931]

New York, December 24, 1931

To Professor Lindemann

Street and No. Christ Church, Oxford, (England)

Many thanks dear Prof now please calculate for me following [.] What is impact or shock to stationary body two hundred pounds of motor car weighing two thousand four hundred pounds traveling [sic] thirty or thirtyfive miles per hour stop [?] This shock I took in my body being carried forward on the cowcatcher until brakes eventually stopped car when I dropped off [.] Brakes did not operate till car hit me stop [.] Want figure for article [.] Think it must be impressive [.] Kindly cable weekend [.] Letter at my expense [.] Am expecting recover completely in month [.] Pretty good [.] Your Friend [.] Winston

Original in capitals with no punctuation

Just received wire [.] Delighted good news stop [.] Collision equivalent falling thirty feet onto pavement [,] equal sixthousand footpounds energy [,] equivalent stopping ten pound brick dropped sixhundred feet or two charges buckshot pointblank range stop [.] Shock presumably proportional rate energy transferred stop [.] Rate inversely proportional thickness cushion surrounding skeleton and give of frame stop [.] If assume average one inch your body transferred during impact at rate eight thousand horsepower stop [.] Congratulations on preparing suitable cushion and skill in taking bump [.] Greetings to all [.]

Lindemann Hotel Continental Nice

[Original in capitals with no punctuation]

An Appeal to Deaf Ears?

The Munich crisis is now seen as a turning point for Churchill. In the years leading up to Munich, he seemed politically isolated and his warnings about the rise of Hitler and his opposition to German rearmament and expansion fell largely on deaf ears. "After Munich it was impossible to dismiss Churchill's speeches as picturesque sabre-rattling."

For a while in the autumn of 1938, Europe seemed close to war. Hitler's latest territorial demand, for the immediate transfer of the German-speaking Sudetenland from Czechoslovakia, led to a tense period of international diplomacy, culminating in a four-power summit meeting between Britain, Germany, France, and Italy in Munich at the end of September. The Czechs had no voice. The Sudetenland was duly annexed, and Prime Minister Neville Chamberlain returned to a rapturous welcome from the relieved British public. Disembarking triumphantly from his aeroplane at Heston, he was pictured waving a piece of paper signed by himself and Chancellor Hitler, "symbolic of the desire of our two peoples never to go to war with one another again," and promising peace "for our time."

Churchill spoke out powerfully against the Munich agreement. First, in the British Parliament on October 5, where he criticized the whole policy of appeasement: "…we have passed an awful milestone in our history, when the whole equilibrium of Europe has been deranged, and that the terrible words have for the time being been pronounced against the Western democracies: 'Thou art weighed in the balance and found wanting.' And do not suppose that this is the end. This is only the beginning of the reckoning."

Then, just over two weeks later, on October 16, 1938, Churchill broadcast directly to the United States on an American radio channel. His message was simple. The New World could no longer afford to ignore what was happening in Europe. There was still time for the English-speaking peoples to stand together and defend democracy against dictatorship.

Churchill's speech notes are of interest in themselves. They provide an insight into his working process. Initially, he would dictate and the speech would be set down in normal typescript by one of a team of personal secretaries. Churchill would then go through the typescripts and make changes, more often than not in his characteristic red pen. When he was happy that the speech was close to its final form, it would be converted from the standard typescript sheets into blank-verse speaking notes. These were the actual pages from which Churchill would deliver the speech or broadcast. Even then, as with this example, Churchill would regularly make last-minute alterations, many of them improvements to the wording or phrasing rather than to the content. He always prepared extremely thoroughly, and the speech notes are almost verbatim, providing both a strong visual reminder for emphasis and an aide-memoire. They are the scripts from which Churchill crafted his drama.

There is no doubt that this particular speech was widely heard in the United States. Many of the letters Churchill received from American listeners survive among his papers. They are revealing and tell us something about how Churchill, Britain, and Munich were seen in the United States. Some are highly supportive. A gentleman in Ohio wrote, "...as Americans, and of course, real lovers of true democracy, we know American frontiers are at the Rhine and our battlefield wherever and whenever democracy is challenged and imperilled." In a similar vein from another gentleman in Chestnut Hill, Philadelphia: "Certainly the time has come when the democracies of the world must hang together or there is a grave danger they may hang separately."

But others were more critical, blaming the British and their government for the mess in which they now found themselves. From Wayland, Massachusetts: "Why ask America's help, however, while the English retain in power a government that set in motion the whole damnable plot, that scuttled the ship of its friends?" And from Philadelphia: "Why should we trust a [British] government who time after time expresses pious platitudes and then walks out on democracies?...American public opinion can and will change from an isolationist view to an active participation in the fight for freedom only when and if it is clearly demonstrated to us that Great Britain and France are willing and wholeheartedly, in that fight."

Then there is the woman from Jacksonville, Florida, who will not forgive the abdication crisis and the British refusal to countenance a royal marriage to an American woman, and the man from New York who sees hypocrisy in British and French arms sales to Hitler and argues that "since England and France have consistently polluted their bed, may the rest of the world see to it that they alone sleep on it!" And these are just a few examples. There does seem to have been some genuine respect and admiration for Churchill, and Anthony Eden is also often mentioned in a positive light, but it is clear, even from this small and unrepresentative sample, that there was no real consensus of support for Britain.

Churchill must have been only too aware that he faced an uphill task. In the speech, he argues that America will not be able to remain isolated forever. He describes his audience as "increasingly involved spectators" and states, "We are left in no doubt where American conviction and sympathies lie; but will you wait until British freedom and independence have succumbed, and then take up the cause when it is three-quarters ruined, yourselves alone?" It was a theme to which he would return again and again in speeches, articles, letters, and telegrams over the course of the next three years.

His first communication to President Franklin Roosevelt after being installed as the new British prime minister is a case in point. Writing on May 15, 1940, Churchill is brutally candid about the precarious nature of the British

We must arm.   *Britain must arm,*
                               America must arm,

If, through an earnest desire for peace,
    we have placed ourselves at a disadvantage,
        we must make up for it by redoubled exertions,

    and, if necessary, by fortitude in suffering.

We shall no doubt arm.

Britain, casting away the habits of centuries,
    will decree national service upon her citizens.

The British people will stand erect,
    and will face whatever may be coming.

But arms - instrumentalities, as President Wilson called them -
    are not sufficient by themselves.

We must add to them the power of ideas.

People say we ought not to allow ourselves
    to be drawn into a theoretical antagonism
        between Nazidom and democracy;
            but the antagonism is here now.

An extract from Winston S. Churchill's notes for his radio broadcast, October 16, 1938,
Churchill Archives Centre, Churchill Papers, CHAR 9/132/75

position: "…But I trust you realise, Mr President, that the voice and force of the United States may count for nothing if they are withheld too long."

[Extract from speaking notes for broadcast to the United States, October 16, 1938]

We must arm. *Britain must arm, America must arm,*
If, through an earnest desire for peace,
    we have placed ourselves at a disadvantage,
        we must make up for it by redoubled exertions,
and, if necessary, by fortitude in suffering.
We shall no doubt arm.
Britain, casting away the habits of centuries,
    will decree <u>national service</u> upon her citizens.
The British people will stand erect,
    and will face whatever may be coming.
But arms – <u>instrumentalities</u>, as President Wilson called them—
    are not sufficient by themselves.
We must add to them the power of ideas.
People say we ought not to allow ourselves
    to be drawn into a theoretical antagonism
        between Nazidom and democracy;
            <u>but the antagonism is here now.</u>

[Underlining and words in italics added by Winston S. Churchill in penci]l

Forging the Atlantic Alliance

It is January 27, 1941. The United Kingdom, now under Churchill's leadership, has survived the Battle of Britain and the Blitz. Yet the situation is still precarious. The Battle of the Atlantic has not been won, Europe is dominated by Nazi Germany, the Luftwaffe is bombing British cities, the Soviet Union is still bound to Germany by the terms of the 1939 Boundary and Friendship Treaty, and the United States is neutral and has not yet committed to the lend-lease program.

Churchill has made repeated public appeals for help to the United States. His speeches are having a clear effect on British morale, but some of his most famous oratory is aimed as much at the American audience. Take, for example, his famous speech of August 20, 1940, which includes the immortal phrase *"Never in the field of human conflict was so much owed by so many to so few."* This address ends with a comment on the significance of increased American naval activity in the western Atlantic: "Undoubtedly this process means that the two great organizations of the English-Speaking democracies, the British Empire and the United States, will have to be somewhat mixed up together in some of their affairs…Like the Mississippi, it just keeps rolling along. Let it roll. Let it roll on full flood…Let it roll on full flood, inexorable, irresistible, benignant, to broader lands and better days."

Imagine, then, the psychological effect of the delivery of the following letter to Churchill. It is handwritten by Franklin Delano Roosevelt, a man who has just been reelected for an unprecedented third term as American president, a man whom Churchill has not met since 1918 (and then only briefly at an occasion that he struggles to recall), but Roosevelt is also the man on whom Churchill pins all real hope of obtaining ultimate victory in his war against Hitler.

The letter reads as follows:

> Dear Churchill
> Wendell Willkie will give you this—He is truly helping to keep politics out
> over here. I think this verse applies to you people as it does to us:
> 'Sail on, oh ship of state!
> Sail on Oh Union strong and great.
> Humanity with all its fears,
> With all the hope of future years
> Is hanging breathless on thy fate'
> As ever yours
> Franklin d Roosevelt

There was clearly much for Churchill to like here. On a personal level, he would have liked the intimacy being shown by Roosevelt: the fact that the president wrote out not only the letter by hand but also the accompanying envelope. The tone of the verse by Longfellow would have appealed to his romantic nature and sense of history. Yet it must have been the political message sent by Roosevelt that pleased Churchill the most. For it was no accident that this letter was being entrusted to Wendell Willkie: the man who had run against Roosevelt as the Republican candidate in the 1940 presidential election, but who shared Roosevelt's views on the need to support Britain. His mission to see Churchill, with this letter of introduction from Roosevelt, was a clear statement of bipartisan support for Britain, and an indication, through its deliberate linking of the British cause with that of the United States, that Roosevelt might now be prepared to offer more than a few old destroyers.

It is clear that Churchill recognized the importance of this document. He chose to reproduce it in the third volume of *The Second World War*, where he commented, "These splendid lines from Longfellow's 'Building of the Ship' were an inspiration," and he immediately telegraphed Roosevelt to say, "I received Willkie yesterday, and was deeply moved by the verse of Longfellow's which you had quoted. I shall have it framed as a souvenir of these tremendous days, and as a mark of our friendly relations, which have been built up telegraphically but also telepathically under all the stresses." The faded appearance of this document, from White House green to brown, is a testament to the fact that Churchill was as good as his word. The letter was framed, and hung for a long time in his beloved house at Chartwell.

Yet Churchill was also a statesman of great experience, and there is no doubt that he recognized not only the long-term historic importance of this letter, but also the short-term political value. It was ammunition that he could turn to his advantage in his ongoing written and oral assault on the hearts and minds of the people of the United States. On February 9 he broadcast to America, ending in typically dramatic fashion by quoting the president's letter back across the Atlantic, with this stirring piece of oratory:

> The other day, President Roosevelt gave his opponent
> in the late Presidential Election
> a letter of introduction to me,
> and in it he wrote out a verse from Longfellow
> which, he said, applies to you people as it does to us.

24.

The other day, President Roosevelt gave his opponent

      in the late Presidential Election,
      a letter of introduction to me,

   and in it he wrote out a verse from Longfellow
   which, he said, "applies to you people as it does to us."

Here is the verse:

      "Sail on, O Ship of State!
      Sail on, O Union, strong and great!
      Humanity with all its fears,
      With all the hopes of future years,
      Is hanging breathless on thy fate! "

What is the answer that I shall give in your name
    to this great man,
      the (head thrice-chosen, of a nation of a hundred and
                               thirty million?

Here is the answer.

Put your confidence in us;

      give us your faith and your blessing,

         and under Providence all will be well.

We shall not fail or falter.

We shall not weaken or tire.

Neither the sudden shock of battle nor the long-drawn
    trials of vigilance and exertion will wear us down.

Give us the tools, and we will finish the job.

An extract from Winston S. Churchill's notes for his radio broadcast, February 9, 1941,
Churchill Archives Centre, Churchill Papers, CHAR 9/1501/51

Churchill then quotes the verse before going on to finish:

> What is the answer that I shall give in your name
> to this great man,
> the head thrice-chosen of a nation of a hundred and thirty million?
> Here is the answer.
> Put your confidence in us;
> give us your faith and your blessing,
> and under Providence all will be well.
> We shall not fail or falter.
> We shall not weaken or tire.
> Neither the sudden shock of battle nor the long-drawn
> trials of vigilance and exertion will wear us down.
> Give us the tools, and we will finish the job.

These are powerful words that still resonate today, and which were quite deliberately echoed by President George W. Bush in his address to Congress in the aftermath of September 11, 2001. Look at the way the original document is laid out, in blank verse, or what Churchill's office called his psalm form. It hints strongly at how important the delivery and emphasis was to Churchill. The message of the speech is clear. On the one hand, it sends a signal to the embattled people of Britain that help will come; on the other, it tells the people of the United States that they must provide it.

Dealing with New Challenges

The friendship between Winston Churchill and President Harry S. Truman had a difficult birth. The sudden death in office of President Franklin Roosevelt in April 1945 deprived Churchill of a close ally and left the British prime minister facing the prospect of negotiating with Stalin alongside a new and, to him at least, relatively unknown quantity in the person of former Vice President Truman.

Things did not begin well. For reasons that are still not altogether clear, Churchill chose not to attend Roosevelt's funeral, thereby losing an early opportunity to meet with Truman. Then Truman suggested, through his ambassador in Britain, that he might meet with Stalin alone prior to the "big three" meeting of the American, Soviet, and British leaders in Potsdam, Germany. Churchill objected in the strongest terms, and Truman withdrew the proposal, but it must have been with some trepidation that the two men approached their first real meeting.

Fortunately, there is every indication that the seeds of mutual appreciation were sown at the Potsdam Conference. On the evening of July 23, Churchill hosted a meal for the American and Russian delegations. He was presented with a signed seating plan as a personal souvenir, with Stalin apparently acting as the autograph hunter. The first signature is that of Harry Truman, and he prefaces it with the simple phrase, "To one of the world's great men." Two days later, Churchill left the conference fully expecting to return. He arrived in Britain to hear the results of the postwar general election, and found the Labour Party victorious and Clement Attlee elected as prime minister in his place.

Churchill was now out of office. That could have been the end of his short relationship with Truman. Yet he remained extremely popular on the international stage, and nowhere more so than in the United States. Truman now played an important role in getting Churchill back on his political feet, by encouraging him to visit the United States and by endorsing an invitation for Churchill to give a lecture at Westminster College, in Fulton, Missouri. The invitation to deliver the Green Lecture was issued by the college president, Dr. F. L. McCluer, but came with a handwritten codicil from Truman: "This is a wonderful school in my home state. Hope you can do it. I'll introduce you."

Truman was better than his word. Not only did he introduce Churchill at Fulton, he also loaned him the presidential plane for a trip to Cuba, and traveled with him on the presidential train to Missouri. In the short term, he may have regretted his close association and generosity. Churchill's speech at Westminster College was a call for closer Anglo-American cooperation, but it immediately became famous for its powerful warning about the Soviet danger in Eastern Europe: "From Stettin in the Baltic to Trieste in the Adriatic an Iron Curtain has descended across the Continent." The speech, with its criticism of the Soviet Union, a wartime ally, caused a sensation, and Truman had to distance himself from it. Yet very quickly, as American relations with the Soviet Union deteriorated, it came to be seen as prophetic, cementing Churchill's reputation, and benefiting President Truman by association.

The personal rapport between Truman and Churchill after the Fulton speech was clearly very close. They wrote some of their letters by hand and addressed one another intimately and informally as Harry and Winston. On May 12, 1947, Churchill wrote to Truman expressing his admiration for "what you have done for the peace and freedom of the world, since we were together." On October 14, Truman wrote, "You are very kind to me, and I think you give me too much credit. But I like it particularly from you." When Truman won the presidential election in 1948, Churchill was fulsome in his praise of "your gallant fight," "tremendous victory," and "personal triumph." And in September 1949, Truman drove out into Maryland to watch Sarah Churchill perform in the Philip Barry play *The Philadelphia Story*, subsequently sending Churchill signed photographs of the occasion.

In this letter of July 10, 1948, written ostensibly to thank Churchill for his gift of the first volume of his war memoirs, *The Gathering Storm*, Truman refers to his election campaign as a "terrible political 'trial by fire.'" He mentions the defeat of Nazism and Fascism and talks of Communism as the next great problem. This captures the nature of the relationship between the two men, a relationship that was born in the final days of World War II and developed against the backdrop of the escalating Cold War.

By the time Truman wrote this letter there had been Soviet takeovers in Hungary, Romania, Poland, and Czechoslovakia. The United States had enacted the Marshall Plan, providing huge amounts of aid to Western Europe in an attempt to limit economic instability and prevent the further spread of Communism. The letter, with its reference to "trying times," was written against the backdrop of the Berlin blockade. The Soviet Union had shut down all overland communication with the American, British, and French zones in Berlin, and this western enclave was being kept alive by an airlift. Just nine

President Harry S. Truman's autograph letter to Winston S. Churchill, July 10, 1948,
Churchill Archives Centre, Churchill Papers, CHUR 2/158/43

months before, in his letter to Churchill of October 14, 1947, Truman had reflected: "Our Russian 'friends' seem most ungrateful for the contribution which your great country and mine made to save them. I sometimes think perhaps we made a mistake—and then I remember Hitler. He had no heart at all. I believe that Joe Stalin has one but the Politbureau won't let him use it."

Like Truman, Churchill continued to wrestle with these problems, returning for a second term as British prime minister in 1951. And there is evidence that he too believed that there was some hope, if only a way could be found of resurrecting the wartime dialogue with Stalin.

[Transcript of Letter from President Truman to Winston S. Churchill, July 10, 1948]

July 10, 1948
The White House
 Washington*

Mrs C to see**

My dear Winston: -
I was deeply touched by your good letter of June 7. I am going through a terrible political "trial by fire". Too bad it must happen at this time.
 Your great country and mine are founded on the fact that the people have the right to express themselves on their leaders, no matter what the crisis.
 Your note accompanying "The Gathering Storm" is highly appreciated and I have made it a part of the book.
 We are in the midst of grave and trying times. You can look with satisfaction upon your great contribution to the overthrow of Nazism + Fascism in the World.
 "Communism"—so called, is our next great problem. I hope we can solve it without the "blood and tears" the other two cost.
 May God bless and protect you.
 Ever sincerely your friend
 Harry Truman

[end of page 2]

Thanks, "a million" for the Gathering Storm.

* Standard printed letterhead
** Added in a different hand. Indicates that the letter was to be shown to Mrs. Churchill

Old Faces and New Realities

As this letter points out, Churchill and General Dwight D. Eisenhower had a long and impressive shared history. The careers of both men were made in the dark days of World War II. Churchill's "finest hour" came in the summer of 1940, when he gave voice to Britain's defiance of Nazi Germany; Eisenhower's came in the summer of 1944, when he successfully launched and led the D-Day landings and the ensuing Allied liberation of Western Europe.

Eisenhower's achievement in holding together the multinational Allied army, an army that included such strong personalities as General George Patton, Field Marshal Bernard Montgomery, and General Charles de Gaulle, was recognized by Churchill. In his telegram to President Truman of May 9, 1945, a message that was clearly intended for wider public consumption, he paid tribute to Eisenhower as "a man who set the unity of the Allied Armies above all nationalistic thoughts. In his Headquarters unity and strategy were the only reigning spirits. The unity reached such a point that British and American troops could be mixed in the line of battle, and that large masses could be transferred from one Command to the other without the slightest difficulty."

It was on the strength of this achievement and with this reputation that the Republican Eisenhower fought and won the presidential election of 1952. By this time Churchill was also back in power as prime minister, his Conservative Party having narrowly won a British general election in October 1951. The two old army officers were now confronted with a new set of international problems. The world was divided into two armed camps: the Western powers and their allies on the one side, the Communist regimes in the Soviet Union and China with their allies on the other. Overshadowing everything was the threat of nuclear war.

Churchill had long been calling for a summit meeting with the Russian leadership. He advocated a return to the type of "big three" diplomacy that had dominated his war premiership. Eisenhower was skeptical and favored a tougher and more rigid anti-Communist stance. In March 1953 Stalin died and Churchill saw a window of opportunity. He persuaded Eisenhower to attend a three-power summit meeting with himself and the French prime minister in Bermuda. Originally scheduled for the summer, the meeting had to be postponed when Churchill suffered a severe stroke, and finally took place in December. Churchill's hopes of breaking the Cold War impasse were dashed. Eisenhower compared the new Soviet leadership to a woman of the streets, saying it did not matter whether her clothes were old or new.

There can be no doubt that Churchill relished reprising his wartime role on the international stage. Yet he was also motivated by a desire to break the stalemate of the Cold War and avert a possible nuclear war. Such an achievement would have crowned his career and established him as a great peacemaker as well as war leader. It was not to be, although several scholars have pointed out that the Bermuda Conference did set the precedent for future Cold War summits.

By the beginning of 1955, Churchill's political powers were failing. He was now eighty years old. His stroke of 1953, though concealed from all but an inner circle, had been severe, and Anthony Eden, foreign secretary once again, was growing tired of playing successor-in-waiting. On March 18, Churchill sent a telegram to Eisenhower in which he reflected that he was sorry that "we shall never meet in a Top level confrontation of our would-be friends." It was a tacit admission that he was about to stand down, and something that cannot have come as a surprise to the White House.

Eisenhower's letter to Churchill touches on both the past and the present. It begins by recalling their common wartime experiences and the great operations they had planned together. TORCH was the codename for the Allied invasion of North Africa in 1942. The text then turns to the difficulties of the present, and the "struggle against the evil conspiracy centering in the Kremlin." It touches on a practical problem arising from the declassification in the United States of papers relating to the 1945 Yalta Conference, papers that were still closed in the United Kingdom. It also comments on the divergence of opinion between Britain and the United States over policy in

Southeast Asia and China. This was a constant theme in communications between the two leaders at this time. Eisenhower could not understand the British unwillingness to back his robust line in support of the Chinese Nationalist leader, Chiang Kai-shek, who was holding Formosa [Taiwan] and various other coastal islands against the Communist forces of the Chinese mainland. Seven days later he would write to Churchill again, complaining that "your own government seems to regard Communist aggression in Asia as of little significance to the free world future."

The letter sheds light on the challenges facing the Anglo-American alliance. It also reveals something of the relationship between Churchill and Eisenhower. Underneath the differences of opinion were shared experiences and mutual admiration. Eisenhower ends by discussing his "portrait." He was attempting to produce a painting of Sir Winston. Churchill, an accomplished artist, was already aware of this and clearly amused. His telegram of March 18, already cited, had contained the following postscript: "How are you getting on with the portrait? I hope you will show it to me when it is finished and I warn you I shall claim full rights of retaliation."

[Transcript of Letter from President Dwight D. Eisenhower to Winston S. Churchill, March 22, 1955]

THE WHITE HOUSE
WASHINGTON

March 22 1955.

TOP SECRET

Dear Winston

The last sentence of your letter, with its implication that you are soon to withdraw from active political life, started, in my memories, a parade of critical incidents and great days that you and I experienced together, beginning at the moment we first met in Washington, December 1941. Since reading it I have been suffering from an acute case of nostalgia.

First I recall those late days of 1941, when this country was still shuddering from the shock of Pearl Harbor. I think of those occasions during the succeeding months when I was fortunate enough to talk over with you some of the problems of the war, and I especially think of that Washington visit of yours in June of '42, when we had to face the bitter reality of the Tobruk disaster.

Somewhere along about that time must have marked the low point in Allied war fortunes. Yet I still remember with great admiration the fact that never once did you quail at the grim prospect ahead of us; never did I hear you utter a discouraged word nor a doubt as to the final and certain outcome.

Later, of course, we were often together as we planned the torch Operation, the Sicilian venture, the move into Italy, and the campaign through Normandy. Then, in these later years, starting with my return to Europe in January of '51, I have valued beyond calculation my opportunities to meet with you, especially when those meetings were concerned with military and diplomatic problems of the free world and our struggle against the evil conspiracy centering in the Kremlin. Because I do so highly value this long association and friendship with you, I echo your hope that the impending divergence of our lives will apply to political occasions only. Indeed, I entertain the further hope that with greater leisure, you will more often find it possible to visit us in this country—after all, we do have a fifty percent share in your blood lines, if not in your political allegiance.

Of course both Foster and I have been unhappy about the affair of the Yalta papers. Actually we had hoped that we had made adequate arrangement for an indefinite postponement of the appearance of the documents; an unexplained leak finally put the State Department in the position that it had either to release the papers publicly or to allow one lone periodical a complete scoop in the matter.

As for myself, you know how earnestly I have argued that no matter what else might happen, really good international friends cannot ever afford to be guilty of bad faith, one toward the other. I pray that you do not consider that any such thing was intended in this case.

Ever since 1945, I have argued for the declassification of war records in order that our countries could profit from past mistakes. But I have also insisted that where documents touch upon our combined alliances and arrangements of the late war, published accounts should be limited to a recitation of fact and decision—they should not include mere conversation or gossip.

I think the entire subject is one to which we should give some attention because I am certain that future political battles will create, in some instances, irresistible demands for the publication of particular papers. At least I suspect that this will be true in this country and consequently I think we should prepare as intelligently as possible for this eventuality.

Foster has just returned from Canada where he had a series of very fine visits with the members of the Canadian Government. While there, he had an opportunity to explain the reasons for our attitude in the Formosa matter.

As you know, I am dedicated to the idea that unless the free world can stand firmly together in important problems, our strength will be wasted and we shall in the long run be ineffective in our struggle to advance freedom in the world and to stop the spread of Communism. I believe it to be especially important that we seek to understand each other's viewpoints in Southeast Asia, because in that region we have a very delicate—sometimes dangerously weak—situation and one to which the future welfare and fortunes of the free world are definitely related. If we can achieve the kind of common under-standing and thinking that we should, then I feel that there will never be any doubts as to this country's readiness to stand firmly by the side of any other free nation opposing aggression in that region. We have no possessions in that immediate area. Consequently, we cannot be accused of any support of colonialism or of imperialistic designs. We recognize situations that have been properly and legally established and we certainly want to halt Communism dead in its tracks.

To do this, one of the essentials is a strong and continuous land defense of Formosa. This can be done—certainly under present conditions—only by Chiang Kai-shek and his troops. This in turn means that their morale and their vigor, their training and equipment, must all be adequately assured. Until the time comes that they themselves feel that their morale can be sustained, even though their forces are withdrawn from all of their outlying positions, we must be exceedingly careful of the pressures we attempt to apply to Chiang to bring about such a result.

FOLLOWING PAGES
President Dwight D. Eisenhower's letter to Winston S. Churchill, March 22, 1955, Churchill Archives Centre, Churchill Papers, CHUR 2/217/25-29

THE WHITE HOUSE
WASHINGTON

March 22, 1955.

Dear Winston

The last sentence of your letter, with its implication that you are soon to withdraw from active political life, started, in my memories, a parade of critical incidents and great days that you and I experienced together, beginning at the moment we first met in Washington, December, 1941. Since reading it I have been suffering from an acute case of nostalgia.

First I recall those late days of 1941, when this country was still shuddering from the shock of Pearl Harbor. I think of those occasions during the succeeding months when I was fortunate enough to talk over with you some of the problems of the war, and I especially think of that Washington visit of yours in June of '42, when we had to face the bitter reality of the Tobruk disaster.

Somewhere along about that time must have marked the low point in Allied war fortunes. Yet I still remember with great admiration the fact that never once did you quail at the grim prospect ahead of us; never did I hear you utter a discouraged word nor a doubt as to the final and certain outcome.

Later, of course, we were often together as we planned the TORCH Operation, the Sicilian venture, the move into Italy, and the campaign through Normandy. Then, in these later years, starting with my return to Europe in January of '51, I have valued beyond calculation my opportunities to meet with you, especially when those meetings were concerned

THE WHITE HOUSE
WASHINGTON

The Prime Minister - 5

Actually, I have not had time to complete every detail of
this particular canvas because I must say that it is difficult
for me to give a fairly realistic impression of the stripes in
a statesman's trousers.   I could wish that, at least for
the day you sat for that portrait, you could have worn your
wartime "zipper suit."

h my affectionate regard and my most prayerful wishes
your continued good health and happiness,

on. Sir Winston Churchill
M., C.H., M.P.
ime Minister
n, England

Except for this one feature, I agree entirely with the thoughts you have expressed in your former letters on this touchy subject, and I hope also that you have no difficulty of seeing the importance of this morale feature in Formosa.

As to the "portrait": Since Mr. Stephens has come back, I have had no opportunity to meet with him to go over the work he did on my behalf. However, in the meantime I discovered a small black and white print of a portrait of you that was painted some years ago. In order to obtain some practice in the task that I had set for myself, I have painted a small canvas, using this photograph as a guide. I do not know the name of the original artist, but it is a picture of you sitting in a straight-backed chair, in a paneled study, and holding a cigar in your right hand. Considering my lack of qualifications in this field, it did not turn out badly and I have had a color photograph made of it, which I am forwarding with this letter.

Actually, I have not had time to complete every detail of this particular canvas because I must say that it is difficult for me to give a fairly realistic impression of the stripes in a statesman's trousers. I could wish that, at least for the day you sat for that portrait, you could have worn your wartime "zipper suit."

With my affectionate regard and my most prayerful wishes for your continued good health and happiness,

as ever
Ike

The Rt. Hon. Sir Winston Churchill
K.G., O.M., C.H., M.P.
The Prime Minister
London, England

[Manuscript additions in italics]

ENDNOTE

These essays can do little more but skim the surface of the huge subjects and personalities they seek to describe. They draw primarily on the Churchill Papers and the range of primary sources held in the Churchill Archives Centre, Churchill College, Cambridge, U.K. For further information about the Centre, including the on-line catalogue to the Churchill Papers, interested parties should access the website at www.chu.cam.ac.uk/archives/.

American readers and researchers not able to have immediate access to the wealth of original documents held by Churchill College may nonetheless consider themselves fortunate enough to have available for consultation the eight-volume official biography *Winston S. Churchill*, by Randolph S. Churchill and Sir Martin Gilbert (Boston, Mass.: Houghton Mifflin, 1966–1988). These works are supplemented by Companion Volumes, including three volumes (to date) edited by Gilbert and published by W.W. Norton as *The Churchill War Papers* (1993–2001). The Companion Volumes reproduce the most important texts from a multitude of different sources. Collectively, Sir Martin's brilliant and monumental works constitute the starting point for all serious study of Winston Churchill.

Many of the documents that have been cited from the Churchill Papers are reproduced and analysed in the official biography. For *Brighton, Buffalo Bill, and the "Boneless Wonder"* see Volume I, Companion I, chapter 4. For *First Impressions of the United States* see Volume I, chapter 8 and Volume I, Companion I, chapter 9. For *West Coast Adventures* see Volume V, chapter 17 and Volume V, Companion II, September 1929. For *A Close Encounter* see Volume V, chapter 22. For *An Appeal to Deaf Ears* see Volume V, chapter 49 and Volume V, Companion III, October 1938 and *The Churchill War Papers* Volume II 'Never Surrender', May 1940. For *Forging the Atlantic Alliance* see *The Churchill War Papers* Volume II, August 1940 and *The War Papers* Volume III 'The Ever Widening War', January 1941. For *Dealing with New Challenges* see Volume VIII, chapters 5 & 10. For *Old Faces and New Realities* see Volume VIII, chapters 47–50.

Churchill and the Great Republic

'Incandescent Quality':
Churchill Materials in the Library of Congress

'Incandescent Quality':
Churchill Materials in the Library of Congress

The Charge of the Twenty-first Lancers

In 1898, at the age of twenty-three, Winston Churchill was a young man in a hurry. He was anxious to make his mark upon the world of British politics and to follow in his father's brilliant though somewhat erratic footsteps. He was perhaps equally anxious to earn money sufficient to enable him and his equally improvident mother to maintain the style of life that they both enjoyed and to which they both felt entitled. Ample funding would also be necessary if Churchill, as he fervently hoped, entered politics and stood for Parliament. Seemingly little could be accomplished while serving as a poorly paid British Army subaltern.

Churchill had already marked out the best approach. Three years earlier he had been an informal military observer and paid newspaper correspondent with Spanish forces trying to suppress insurgents in Cuba. In 1897 he had with some difficulty attached himself to an expedition to subdue rebellious tribes on the northwest frontiers of India; from this excursion came Churchill's first book, *The Story of the Malakand Field Force*. Early in 1898 his efforts to see combat with a similar campaign, the Tirah Expedition, proved fruitless: a peace was negotiated soon after Lieutenant Churchill maneuvered his way onto a general's staff.

Undeterred, Churchill began to focus on an even better opportunity. In 1896 British Empire forces, charged with the reconquest of the Sudan, had begun a methodical campaign up the Nile. Their destination was Khartoum, where the temporal and spiritual leader of the Sudanese, the Mahdi, had killed the fabled British general Charles George "Chinese" Gordon eleven years before. Churchill badgered his acquaintances and urged his mother to use her many important contacts to secure him a position with the Anglo-Egyptian force led by General H. Herbert Kitchener, the "Sirdar" (commander-in-chief) of the Egyptian army. Kitchener resisted, but Churchill's persistence, together with the efforts of Sir Evelyn Wood, the adjutant general of the British Army, resulted in a posting with the Twenty-first Lancers. He also made an agreement with the London *Morning Post* to write newspaper articles about the fighting. He joined his new unit shortly before the climactic battle of the entire campaign took place outside the city of Omdurman, the capital of the Mahdist ("Dervish") kingdom, just across the White Nile from Khartoum.

On September 2, 1898, Kitchener's modern weapons and overwhelming firepower destroyed the Mahdist army with, for the most part, minimal losses to his own forces. Churchill's Twenty-first Lancers were not so fortunate. Deployed to cut off the enemy's line of retreat, they came under fire from their right flank, where, it was thought, a few hundred riflemen had established themselves. Wheeling about and charging their tormentors, they quickly discovered that they had ridden into the midst of a much larger Mahdist force located in a shallow depression. The Lancers incurred seventy-one casualties, including twenty-one killed, out of a total force of 310—losses so heavy as to jeopardize accomplishment of their traditional cavalry missions. After the battle Kitchener sent the unit northward toward Cairo, Alexandria, and Britain. Churchill traveled with them for a while and then journeyed on his own toward London. He began this letter of September 29 to his cousin "Sunny," the ninth Duke of Marlborough, while riding on the train in Austria. He finished it a few days later, as his postscript indicates, in his London home, after teasing Marlborough for using the somewhat formal abbreviation "MM" (for Majesties) on his envelope.

To his cousin, who was also his friend and would become his political colleague and benefactor, the young combat veteran wrote of many things.

First and perhaps most pressing were his family finances, with which Marlborough had evidently offered to help. Next came a capsule description of the Battle of Omdurman, an experience about which Churchill was ambivalent. He gloried in the comparison of his unit's efforts with those of the Light Brigade at Balaclava, and praised the enemy's courage. He also admitted, however, that he had "seen acts of great barbarity perpetrated at Omdurman and have been thoroughly sickened of human blood."

The most striking portions of Churchill's letter accused General Kitchener, by then a national hero, of war crimes, poor leadership, and bad manners. He admitted that Kitchener had performed brilliantly as a strategic and logistic planner (much like François-Michel le Tellier, Marquis de Louvois, minister of war under the French monarch Louis XIV), but Churchill gave more credit for tactical prowess to Kitchener's subordinate, General Archibald Hunter (whom he compared to Louis II de Bourbon, Prince of Condé, another great French general of the seventeenth century). Although he promised to keep his personal feelings to himself, his animus against Kitchener would become evident when, a year later, he published his two-volume memoir/history, entitled *The River War; An Historical Account of the Reconquest of the Soudan*. Retired army colonel Francis W. Rhodes, who served as correspondent during the campaign for *The Times* of London (and whose brother was the famed colonialist Cecil Rhodes, founder of the Rhodes scholarships), gathered materials for Churchill and edited the volume.

Churchill was as excited about his political prospects as he was about his prospective authorship. In July 1898 he had addressed a political meeting in the West Yorkshire city of Bradford; the experience, he told Marlborough, was the "greatest pleasure" of his life. After leaving the army he made a political speech in Birmingham the following June in which, although he commented unfavorably on the behavior of the British Army in the aftermath of the Omdurman victory, he defended Kitchener from the charge of having dese-

Winston S. Churchill's autograph letter to his cousin, the Duke of Marlborough, after the Battle of Omdurman, September 29, 1898, Library of Congress, Washington, D.C., Manuscript Division, Marlborough Mss., 1:44

In the train
near Vienna
29. Sept. 1898

My dear Jummy,

I shall set my pencil against your typewriter,
If you forgive the one as readily as I forgive the
other we shall not quarrel. I telegraphed to
London to have my letters forwarded to Trieste,
but yours was the only one of any consequence
that reached me. That was however so agreeable
to read and to receive that I knew no disappointment. "after compliments" let me proceed.

It is very good of you to say that
you will help me in the financial affair.
I am grateful not only from the material
point of view but also because I appreciate
the fact that you regard me with affection
I am coming home for at least a
month and shall go thoroughly into
the whole state of my mother's business
and my own. Both are small but
tangled. I am at present very ignorant
of the details. When I have mastered the
whole affair & had sought out a
plan I will talk it over with you
& you shall say what you recommend
and what you are to do. There is
no longer any element of hurry. I was
anxious to have the matter settled
before the climax of the London operations
as had I been killed the money of the
Insurance would have been of use
to Jack and my mother. That
eventuality is one which I need not
now contemplate. I therefore leave the
business matters until I have some
opportunity of doing as I have said above.

crated the Mahdi's tomb. By then he was actively campaigning for a seat in Parliament. His defeat in the July 1899 elections marked only a temporary setback in one of the most remarkable political careers of modern times.

Finally, Churchill reflected upon his good fortune. He rejoiced in his prospects and admitted that luck had played a large part in his survival. He had arrived in Egypt too late to take command of the cavalry troop that had been led at the charge by his friend Robert Grenfell. Grenfell had been killed. Another friend, Richard Molyneux, sustained a severe sword cut during hand-to-hand fighting and only narrowly escaped death. Churchill was not, however, destined to be buried "in that hot red sand at Omdurman."

[Transcript of letter from Winston S. Churchill to the Duke of Marlborough, September 29, 1898]

In the train
Near Vienna

My Dear Sunny,

I shall set my pencil against your typewriter. If you forgive the one as readily as I forgive the other we shall not quarrel. I telegraphed to London to have my letters forwarded to Trieste, but yours was the only one of any consequence that reached me. That was however so agreeable to read and to receive that I knew no disappointment. "After compliments" let me proceed.

It is very good of you to say that you will help me in the financial affair. I am grateful not only from the material point of view but also because I appreciate the fact that you regard me with affection. I am coming home for at least a month and shall go thoroughly into the whole state of my mother's business and my own. Both are small but tangled. I am at present very ignorant of the details. When I have mastered the whole affair & have roughed out a plan I will talk it over with you & you shall say what you recommend and what you care to do. There is no longer an element of hurry. I was anxious to have the matter settled before the climax of the Soudan operations as had I been killed the money [with] the insurance would have been of use to Jack and to my mother. That eventuality is one which I need not now contemplate. I therefore leave the business matters until I have had some opportunity of doing as I have said above.

Now about the war: - Perhaps you will read my letters in the "Morning Post". They contain the best of my impressions put down as carefully, from the point of view of style, as I can. The military operations, though short, have been interesting. The Battle was a wonderful spectacle. ~~The~~ I had the good luck to ride through the charge unhurt–indeed untouched–which very few can say. I used a pistol and did not draw my sword. I had no difficulties and felt confident that I should get through if, neither my horse fell nor I was shot—for I must tell you the ground was execrable and there was the wildest shooting in all directions. Neither of these things happened and such of the enemy as approached me or attacked me I shot—three I think I killed. It is difficult to miss at under a foot's range. The whole thing was a matter of seconds—for as you may have gathered—we burst through their line and formed up the other side. The loss was most severe—1 officer and 21 men killed—9 officers and 66 men wounded and 119 horses out of only 320. Such a proportion and such a loss has been sustained by no regiment since the Light Brigade—forty years ago.

Leaving personal matters I would like to write to you about the Sirdar and about the whole conduct of the campaign. But if I embarked on such a voyage I should never get to the end. I am going to write an article called "Reflections on the Expeditions to Khartoum & Tirah" which will contain some criticisms and many comparisons, and the general ~~drift~~ tone of which will be calculated to depreciate diminish the inflated reputation which Sir H. Kitchener has acquired. I do not mean that such will be my intention or that such a result will follow the article. I mean only that the gist of my argument will tend to show that whereas the campaign in Tirah was the hardest ever fought, the campaign on the Nile was the easiest.

I try to be fair and not to allow my personal feelings to bias my judgment—but my dear Sunny, the Sirdar's utter indifference to the sufferings of his own wounded—his brutal orders & treatment with regard to the Dervish wounded—the shameless executions after the victory and the general callousness which he has repeatedly exhibited—have disgusted me. I have seen more war than most boys my age—probably more than any. I am not squeamish, but I have seen acts of great barbarity perpetrated at Omdurman and have been thoroughly sickened of human blood. I shall always be glad that I was one of those who took these brave men on with weapons little better than theirs and with only our discipline to back against their numbers. All the rest of the army merely fed out death by machinery.

If I am to commit myself to an opinion of Sir H. Kitchener I will say—He is a great man, with the power of making up his mind & of coming to great decisions. A man of unquestioned courage—of extraordinary memory foresight and organizing power—of unconquerable patience and perseverance—but a thoroughly bad tactician, ill-mannered, utterly callous, and probably equally unscrupulous.

He has been the Louvois of the war. General Hunter the Prince de Conde. He can put an army on the spot. But those who know him best say that he is a bad hand at moving troops in the presence of the enemy. His extraordinary tactics at Omdurman very nearly led to a disaster and were the laughingstock of the camp.

I wonder whether you will distrust the value of my opinion when I tell you that he detests me and has expressed himself freely on the subject—that he refused to have me with his Egyptian Army at any price—that he was furious with Sir Evelyn Wood for sending out in spite of him—that my remarks on the condition & treatment of our wounded officers & men were reported to him and that every petty annoyance that ingenuity could suggest was obtruded on me in return.

Perhaps you would make certain deductions. I do myself.

I do not propose to take up the pen of the historian to redress the wrongs of the soldier. I intend to write a history of the whole of the re-conquest of the Soudan—1896, 1897, 1898. Frankie Rhodes who knows all the generals and can collect facts is going to edit the book—Longmans will publish. I shall call it "A History of the River-War." If you will allow me I will dedicate it to you. But I shall keep my personal feelings to myself and shall aim only at recording the truth–and when all has been said—the truth is very brilliant and glorious.

I leave the Nile—I have drunk it—floated on it—seen it—washed in it—thought about it, talked about it until I am tired of it.

Politics—I like the idea of an autumn campaign. I suppose the big politicos will all take the field. I propose to deliver several harangues and am accumulating material. I do hope you will help me in some way. The idea of being given a dinner by the Birmingham Conservative Club is v[er]y dear to me. I shall be in England all October—perhaps I shall not go back to India. I should appreciate the honour v[er]y much. Bradford— I mean to go to—I told them I would come back after the Union Jack was hoisted at Khartoum.

You will see by all this—I am still full of vitality and energy. I only look for outlets. It is good to be able to look out on life again, without the feeling that perhaps death impended in the near future. I should have hated to lie in that hot red sand at Omdurman—after all the army had marched away. And yet on what do these things depend. Chance—Providence—God—the Devil—call it what you will. Had I started when I meant to from London I should have had Grenfell's troop and ridden where he rode. I could not get a place in the sleeping car and delayed two days. Whatever it may be—I do not complain—my luck has been "set fair".

Dick Molyneux is coming home with me—a shocking sword cut on his right arm. He is such a good chap and we have made great friends. He tells me he knows you. I shall see you soon.

Yours affectionately,

Winston S. Churchill

P.S. I noticed the "M M" on the envelope. You are quite right. This is not an age in which to let such distinctions die out. Besides alliteration is always popular.

WSC

A line to say I am now at Cumberland Place

WSC

The Road to Fame

In 1899 Churchill's ambitions for fame and fortune suffered a minor setback that, paradoxically, set in motion a train of events that would lead to political success and a seat in the British Cabinet. After returning from the Sudan the previous year, he had gone back to India to complete his career in the army. He then went home to England, where he stood for election to Parliament as a Conservative for Oldham. He made a respectable showing, but his third-place finish forced him to return to his previous career path.

Fortunately for him, an opportunity soon presented itself. In South Africa the British Empire had for some time been in conflict with the two adjacent, independent, and Dutch-speaking "Boer" republics. By the summer of 1899 negotiations between the British and the Boers over voting rights for Britons resident in the republics had broken down. Faced with a build-up of

British military forces and fearing a possible attack, the Boers struck first and invaded British territory.

Churchill, now a civilian war correspondent for the London *Morning Post*, arrived at the seat of war soon after swift-moving and surprisingly effective Boer forces had defeated their British opponents and driven them back into the small town of Ladysmith, in the southeastern colony of Natal. He accepted an officer's offer to ride along in an armored train on a reconnaissance mission toward the besieged city. After the Boers ambushed the small British detachment, Churchill, under withering enemy fire, led a group of volunteers who cleared a derailed car from the tracks, thus allowing the engine to retreat to safety with the wounded. Returning to rejoin the main body of soldiers, Churchill fell into enemy hands and was taken, as a prisoner of war, to Pretoria. Becoming aware of his identity and of the active role he had taken to rescue the hard-pressed soldiers, his captors refused to release him despite his repeated entreaties. Desperate, Churchill then took matters into his own hands and escaped. Alone, far behind enemy lines, with a price on his head for capture dead or alive, Churchill somehow managed to make his way hundreds of miles to the Portuguese colony of Mozambique. From there he took passage on a ship back to friendly territory.

His arrival in Durban on December 23, 1899, was greeted with the greatest enthusiasm, both in England and by the British residents in South Africa. Hailed as a hero at a time when defeats at the hands of the Boers had shaken British confidence, he met with General Sir Redvers Buller, the commander of the forces trying to lift the siege of Ladysmith. Buller commended Churchill for his exploits and asked him whether there was anything he desired in return. Quickly, Churchill requested an officer's commission in one of the irregular units being formed to match the Boer mounted infantry units. This Buller was delighted to agree to, but there remained the question of extracurricular journalistic activities for the *Morning Post*. Churchill's earlier published reports from the Sudan had resulted in a special rule, one forbidding British soldiers from moonlighting as war correspondents. After

Courtesy Charles Scribner's Sons

WINSTON CHURCHILL in 1900, a member of The South African Light Horse during the Boer War.

slight hesitation, Buller waived the rule for the young celebrity and commissioned him a lieutenant in the South African Light Horse. The position, as shown in the photograph taken of Churchill, merited a special khaki uniform, complete with bush hat and decorative plume from the long-tailed sakabula (widow) bird. The optional mustache was added in a mostly unnecessary, and somewhat unsuccessful, attempt to look adventurous and dashing.

Churchill remained as a fighting correspondent in South Africa for several more months, thrilling British readers with his accounts of battle (and of his own daring exploits) and the army's laborious progress toward an imperial victory. He was soon joined at the seat of war by his irrepressible mother, Lady Randolph Churchill, who had raised money for an Anglo-American hospital ship (the *Maine*), and by his younger brother, Jack, for whom he secured a commission in his irregular cavalry unit. On hand for the capture of Pretoria and the liberation of the prison camp from which he had escaped earlier, Churchill's early dispatches to the *Morning Post* were collected and published as a book *(London to Ladysmith Via Pretoria)* while he was still in Africa. At the end of major combat operations he returned to England, landing at Southampton on July 20, 1900. Five days later the Conservatives of Oldham adopted him as one of their candidates for the coming general election—the aptly named "khaki election," in which patriotic support for the war was a decisive factor. This second attempt to replicate his father's electoral career was successful. Churchill was to remain in Parliament, with only a few minor gaps, for six decades.

Teddy and Winnie

Theodore Roosevelt and Winston Churchill had much in common. Temperamentally, they were similar: both were energetic, outspoken, ambitious, adventurous, courageous, and highly intelligent. Both were gifted and prolific writers, and both were talented amateur historians. Each man had first seen military combat in Cuba: Churchill in 1895 (with the Spanish forces trying to put down a rebellion), and Roosevelt in 1898 (with American irregulars trying to defeat those same Spanish troops). The upper-class background that they shared, at least to a certain extent, was supplemented by a kindred desire to right injustices and improve the lot of common men and women. Colorful and controversial, they both captured the imagination of the public and provided the newspapers of the United States and the United Kingdom with a steady stream of good stories.

One thing they did not have in common, however, was mutual admiration—at least on Roosevelt's side. Churchill had met Roosevelt, then governor of New York and vice president-elect, during his 1900–1901 lecture tour of the United States and Canada. According to one account, Churchill's constant cigar smoking and poor manners irritated Roosevelt; his air of self-confidence, or possibly a perceived self-centeredness, may have contributed to the Rough Rider's distaste. Another possibility is that Roosevelt's dislike may have been fueled by the younger man's well-publicized military exploits, which could have threatened to eclipse Roosevelt's equally famous exploits at San Juan Hill (actually Kettle Hill). In a 1901 letter about Churchill's book recounting his earlier adventures with the Malakand Field Force, for example, Roosevelt described the Englishman as "not an attractive fellow," who nonetheless had some interesting things to say.

A similar competitive spirit may have been present in the letter of May 23, 1908, from Roosevelt, then president, to his son Theodore Junior. The younger Roosevelt had mentioned Churchill's recently published two-volume

Page from the Theodore Roosevelt Letterbook, Library of Congress, Washington, D.C., Manuscript Division

May 23, 1908.

Dear Ted:

It gave me quite a pang to receive your letter and feel that you
are really making up your mind to what you are going to do next fall.
Of course I feel sad to think of the little bear going out into the world
at last with a good many troubles and hard times before him.   But you
will be twenty-one, Ted; you want to make your own way, and I have the
utmost confidence and belief in you, and indeed, am very proud of you;
and I am sure you will succeed.   It will be hard at first,
especially when you are working at your utmost, while Kermit and I,
eaten alive with ticks, horse-flies, jiggers, and the like, are enjoying
ourselves in Africa.   The only thing will be to remember that you have
had first-rate fun as a boy up to the time you were twenty-one, and that
the man who is to succeed must buckle to his work during the early
and most important years of his manhood.

Yes, that is an interesting book of Winston Churchill's about his
father; but I can't help feeling about both of them that the older one
was a rather cheap character, and that the younger one is a rather cheap
character.   Recently I have been reading my usual odd variety of books,
including for the last three or four nights Creasy's History of the
Ottoman Turks, which gave me much comfort.   I had a very nice note from
the Brunners in acknowledgment of the volumes I sent on.

David Gray was here this week.   Both Roswell and Audrey are laid
up, much to my disappointment;   but good Bob Bacon gave David Gray a

biography of his father, Lord Randolph Churchill. Roosevelt, who had published several biographies of his own, replied that the book was "interesting," but that he could not "help feeling about both of them that the older one *was* a rather cheap character, and that the younger one *is* a rather cheap character." To another correspondent, Roosevelt would denounce "Churchill's clever, forceful, rather cheap and vulgar life of that clever, forceful, rather cheap and vulgar egoist, his father." Admitting to Senator Henry Cabot Lodge that his "dislike" for both Churchills may have "prejudiced" him, he wrote that both father and son possessed "such levity, lack of sobriety, lack of permanent principle, and an inordinate thirst for that cheap form of admiration which is given to notoriety, as to make them poor public servants."

Published reports of Churchill's African hunting trip, undertaken in 1907 while he was under secretary of state for the colonies, also prompted Roosevelt's desire to equal or excel the younger man's prowess. The president, who planned to undertake a similar trip as soon as he left office in 1909, had read Churchill's account as it had appeared in *The Strand* magazine and was particularly envious of the description of his successful hunt in Uganda for a rare white rhinoceros. In November 1908 he wrote his friend Whitelaw Reid, the U.S. ambassador to the United Kingdom, "Now I should consider my entire African trip a success if I could get to that country and find the game as Churchill describes it." Reid sent him a copy of Churchill's book *My African Journey* by diplomatic pouch as soon as it appeared, followed by a second, specially bound copy, given by the author himself. Placed under an obligation, Roosevelt wrote Reid, "I do not like Winston Churchill but I suppose I ought to write him." His letter of thanks for the present ended with a line about his "proposed trip to Africa." "I trust," Roosevelt said, "I shall have as good luck as you had." The ex-president did in fact get his prized trophies, and after his trip he boasted to the British politician George Otto Trevelyan that he had made a better impression with the British colonials he had encountered than had Churchill: "For various reasons most of them had disliked him when he passed through the country."

Roosevelt finally came to appreciate Churchill's virtues in 1914, after a British friend told him of Churchill's energetic preparations and aggressive actions as first lord of the admiralty at the outbreak of World War I. Roosevelt replied: "I have never liked Winston Churchill, but in view of what you tell me as to his admirable conduct and nerve in mobilizing the fleet, I do wish that if it comes in your way you would extend to him my congratulations on his action."

Redemption by Fire: World War I

During World War I Winston Churchill's career seemingly hit its lowest point. In 1914, as first lord of the admiralty, he had mobilized the British fleet and taken decisive steps to gain and hold command of the seas. During the following year, however, he had sent a naval expedition to Turkey in an ambitious attempt to end the horrifying stalemate on the western front. His battleships were unable to force their way through the Dardanelles Strait to Constantinople (now Istanbul), and the land forces put ashore on the Gallipoli Peninsula to help clear the way became bogged down in a small-scale and very bloody replication of the trench warfare in France and Flanders.

Churchill was widely blamed. Prime Minister Herbert Asquith formed a new government, one in which the services of his controversial first lord were no longer required. Given an anachronistic and largely powerless post, Churchill continued to give advice on the central committee directing the course of the war—the Dardanelles Committee—but he lost all ability to act independently or to see that his ideas on strategy and weaponry were put into effect. The effect on the energetic ex-minister was devastating: his wife, Clementine, later said, "I thought he would die of grief." Frustrated and humiliated, Churchill left the government (but kept his seat in Parliament) on November 11, 1915. He had decided to join the British Army fighting on the western front.

Reporting to General Headquarters, he was offered the command of a brigade by an old friend, Field Marshal Sir John French, the commander of the British Expeditionary Force. Political opponents back in England raised objections to this move, even though Churchill had extensive military experience, both in combat and as a reservist. A further setback occurred on December 15, when Field Marshal Kitchener, Churchill's former commander and colleague, who was then serving as secretary of state for war, fired French and replaced him with General Douglas Haig. Churchill canceled his order for a brigadier general's tunic and, having already served an orientation tour with a front-line Guards unit, took command of the Sixth Battalion of the Royal Scots Fusiliers, in the Ninth (Scottish) Division, as a lieutenant colonel.

Energetic as always, Churchill shared his men's dangerous life and tried to ease their discomforts even as he led them by force of personal example. He endured artillery fire and participated in nighttime reconnaissances. Fortunately, his luck in battle held: he survived a number of near misses, and his service at the front did not coincide with any of the brutally direct assaults undertaken by the British Army against the well-entrenched Germans. After half a year, Churchill's battalion was consolidated with another, one that had an officer senior to him as commander. Out of a job, he could and did leave the fighting with honor and return to London and physically less dangerous pursuits. Among these were service in Parliament; sustained attempts to justify his role in the Dardanelles fiasco; and, after his sometime ally David Lloyd George became prime minister, a fitting outlet for his energies when he became minister of munitions in July 1917. In this position Churchill worked closely with his American counterpart, Bernard Baruch, to coordinate the war production of the United States and the United Kingdom until the conflict finally ended on November 11, 1918.

After two months in action, Churchill wrote his cousin "Sunny" Marlborough on January 12, 1916, while he was getting the men of his new command ready for their rotation in the front-line trenches. He tried to entice Marlborough to come over for a visit, adding that the British Expeditionary

Winston S. Churchill's autograph letter to his cousin, the Duke of Marlborough, from the Western Front, January 12, 1916, Library of Congress, Washington, D.C., Manuscript Division, Marlborough Mss., 2:178

12 . 1 . 16

My dear Sunny,

Your ~~next~~ letter was ~~so~~ welcomed so also will be the food box when it arrives. I don't think it will be impossible to arrange for you to pay me a visit in say 3 weeks time & to stay with us here for a few days – where you will find it interesting & not uncomfortable. But everything must be settled on the right lines. Macready begged me to apply to him ~~to~~ if I wanted a visitor and assured me he will gladly ~~~~ make things smooth. So if you really do like to come let me know & I will approach these deities with the appropriate ritual & genuflexions, when I doubt not they will be favourably disposed.

Of course French's departure has been a most serious loss to me. Haig tho' friendly is not an acquaintance, & I don't expect that he will court any criticism on my account. Why should he? The life of an Infantry Colonel in the line is not at all unpleasant. Creature comforts are not lacking, & everyone in the battalion is of course only anxious to serve & please. There is a constant spice of danger. Daily shells: some of near; & a certain amount of risk in moving about by day and night. I went to see an Artillery strafe two days ago, with my friend of Bangalore days General Tudor who commands

178

Force's adjutant general, Sir Cecil Macready, would be only too pleased to make the necessary arrangements. There were, Churchill added, certainly sights to be seen; he had recently witnessed an artillery duel ("sträfe") in company with Brigadier General Henry Tudor, another old friend from Churchill's days as a subaltern in India.

Churchill's mind was on both danger and destiny. Fatalistic but not pessimistic, he was already planning to speak out in Parliament on the grand strategy of the war, which he felt was being mismanaged by the Asquith government. He was appalled that the Allies were playing into the hands of the Germans and destroying a generation of leaders and builders in the process. A sense of responsibility, however, kept him at the front, at least for the time being, even though he knew it might result in his death. He asked Sunny if he merited the family motto of the first Duke of Marlborough, which they both shared: "faithful but unfortunate [*fiel pero desdichado*]." He closed his letter by marveling that he was now undergoing a trial "quite beyond" any that his father, Lord Randolph Churchill, had undergone.

[Transcript of letter from Winston S. Churchill to Marlborough, January 12, 1916]

6th ROYAL SCOTS FUSILIERS

IN THE FIELD

My dear Sunny,

Your ~~most~~ letter was v[er]y welcome & so also will be the food box when it arrives. I don't think it will be impossible to arrange for you to pay me a visit in say 3 weeks time & to stay with us here for a few days - wh[ich] you will find v[er]y interesting & not uncomfortable. But everything must be settled on the right lines. Macready begged me to apply to him for if I wanted a visitor and assured me he w[oul]d gladly ~~facilitate~~ make things smooth. So if you really w[ould]d like to come let me know & I will approach these deities with the appropriate ritual and genuflections, when I doubt not they will be favorably disposed.

Of course French's departure has been a most serious loss to me. Haig tho[ugh] friendly is only an acquaintance, & I don't expect that he will court any criticism on my account. Why sh[oul]d he? The life of an

Infantry Colonel in the line is not at all unpleasant. Creature comforts are not lacking, & everyone in the battalion is of course very anxious to serve and please. There is a constant spice of danger. Daily shells, some very near; & a certain amount of risk in moving about by day and night. I went to see an artillery sträfe two days ago, with my friend of Bangalore days, General Tudor, who commands the artillery of this division. For one hour by the clock we were involved in a sharp cannonade and I suppose certainly a score of shells burst within 30 yards of us, covering us with dirt and débris. I have also had my tiny dog hole where I sleep in the line smashed up by a shell wh[ich] had it ~~burst properly~~ detonated perfectly w[oul]d have been the end of my chequered fortunes. One becomes quite reconciled to the idea of annihilation & death seems to be divested of any element of tragedy. The only thing to dread is some really life wrecking wound which left one a cripple, an invalid, or an idiot. But that one must hope is not on the agenda of the Fates.

I have meditated a great deal on the g[rea]t situation & have fairly clear views about it. Perhaps later in the year I shall come back to the House: but for the moment this is the course marked out for me. I see no reason to expect a Brigade for a long time & of course there can be no question of any military career. On the other hand, I like soldiering for its own sake; & if I am killed at the head of my battalion, it will be an honourable & dignified finâle. Do you think I sh[oul]d deserve the family motto "Fiel pero desdichado"? I am now passing through a stage in my journey quite beyond any that my father had to traverse. Your letters & affection are a g[rea]t pleasure to me. We must always try to keep together as the world grows grey.

Yours always

W.

The Atlantic Conference

As World War II approached the end of its second year, in the summer of 1941, the outlook for the United Kingdom was bleak. The Germans, having driven the British from Greece and overrun the Balkans, held sway over most of the European continent. They were also making inroads into North Africa, threatening the British Empire's line of communication to India and beyond, and with their submarines were endangering Britain's commercial and logistic lifelines in the Atlantic.

To be sure, this picture was lightened by two factors that promised hope for eventual victory. After June 22, the worst threat of all—invasion—became far less imminent as the Nazis turned their massive forces eastward and invaded the Soviet Union. As the Battle of the Atlantic raged, President Franklin D. Roosevelt was gradually adopting a belligerent posture against the Axis; he was also beginning to establish a personal working alliance with Churchill. In 1939, soon after the war started in Europe, Roosevelt had initiated a correspondence with Churchill, then first lord of the admiralty, and these messages had continued after Churchill became prime minister during the darkest days of the war. Together they had worked out the arrangements for transferring badly needed American escort vessels to the United Kingdom—the destroyers-for-bases deal of September 1940—and had authorized the secret military staff discussions that started the following January. In March 1941 the president signed the lend-lease bill, which in effect provided the British (and later the Soviet Union) with great quantities of war supplies without calling for immediate repayment or politically troublesome loans. Escorting merchant ships bound in convoys to and from the British Isles was an equally touchy political problem, one whose solution Roosevelt preferred to implement gradually. In 1939 he had begun by establishing a "neutrality patrol" to keep belligerents—German submarines and surface raiders—away from the Western Hemisphere. Hemispheric boundaries were eventually expanded to include Greenland, Iceland, and islands in the Azores.

Roosevelt and Churchill had desired a personal meeting since the beginning of 1941, but circumstances had conspired to delay it. Early in the year, Roosevelt was working hard to see lend-lease legislation through Congress. Later, the desperate situation of British forces in Greece and Crete prevented Churchill from leaving his post. Finally the two leaders, with the assistance of Roosevelt emissary Harry Hopkins, agreed upon a time and place. Churchill headed toward the new U.S. base at Argentia, Newfoundland, on board the HMS *Prince of Wales*, a battleship that still bore the scars from its fight against the German battleship *Bismarck* (and that would, in December, be

Franklin D. Roosevelt and Winston S. Churchill meet aboard the U.S.S. *Augusta*, Placentia Bay, Newfoundland, August 9, 1941, Library of Congress, Washington, D.C., Manuscript Division

sunk by the Japanese). Roosevelt, in contrast, set forth on an ostensible fishing trip on board the presidential yacht *Potomac* and then stealthily boarded an American navy vessel. In order to deceive the press, the *Potomac* continued on its pleasure cruise; a double was recruited for the occasion to pose as the president, complete with FDR's trademark cigarette holder.

On August 9 the two men met on board the U.S. Navy cruiser *Augusta*, in Placentia Bay, near the Argentia base. This picture shows the president relying on his leg braces (hidden beneath his trouser legs) for support as he stands, unaided, to shake Churchill's hand; in photographs taken minutes later he is shown leaning on the arm of his son Elliott, a U.S. Army Air Force lieutenant. Another son, Ensign Franklin D. Roosevelt, Jr., is seen standing to the president's right.

This was not their first meeting. In 1918 Roosevelt, then assistant secretary of the navy, had encountered Churchill in England. Churchill had no memory of the encounter but had on this occasion brought with him a letter from King George VI, who had expressed his pleasure that the two leaders were going to confer and had commended his prime minister to Roosevelt as a "very remarkable man."

The Placentia Bay meetings went reasonably well. Roosevelt and Churchill came to know each other better, and their top military and naval leaders continued the pattern of high-level collaboration that would characterize their relationship from that time until the end of the war. Churchill was disappointed at Roosevelt's failure to take more forceful action against Germany, and to use more forceful words against Japan, but American reluctance to move faster toward war could not have been unanticipated. The most publicized result of the conference, the Atlantic Charter, publicly set forth the war aims of the two nations. It committed them both to refrain from territorial aggrandizement, and it pledged their adherence to principles of peace, national self-determination, freedom of the seas, freedom from "fear and want," open access (within limits) to trade and raw materials, improved labor standards, disarmament of aggressor nations, and "a wider and permanent system of general security."

Equally important, perhaps, was the symbolism involved in the leaders of the two great democracies meeting to combat Fascist aggression. The emotional highlight of the meetings was the Sunday religious service held under the guns of the *Prince of Wales* and attended by both the leaders and ordinary sailors from the two English-speaking nations. The event was carefully scripted in advance by Churchill, who chose such hymns as "Onward Christian Soldiers" and "Eternal Father, Strong to Save" (the U.S. Navy hymn, as well as one of Roosevelt's favorites). Churchill wrote later, "It was a great hour to live."

VELVET and the Second Front

By August 1942, the war had reached a crucial stage. The Soviets had managed to stop the invading German armies at the gates of Moscow and Leningrad (St. Petersburg) during the previous winter, but Adolf Hitler's forces had recovered from the Red Army's counter-attacks and had inflicted heavy losses in return. Soviet dictator Josef Stalin had prepared for an anticipated thrust against his capital, but the Germans surprised him in the early summer of 1942 by attacking in the south, toward the Caspian Sea, the Caucasus oilfields, and the strategically important city of Stalingrad. Churchill, an ardent anti-Communist who had tried unsuccessfully to destroy the emerging Bolshevik state after World War I, had promised to assist the Soviets in their struggle, and the United States had joined him in his pledge. The provision of such aid, however, had been rendered problematic by shipping shortages, German attacks, and Anglo-American military requirements.

Desperate, Stalin pressed his allies for a second front in northwest Europe, one that would draw off large numbers of Axis troops. The Americans, who had entered the war in December 1941, favored direct confrontations at decisive points. They were willing to launch such an assault as a means to keep the Soviet Union from outright defeat, or from negotiating a separate peace with the Nazis. The British, who had been driven off the Continent in 1940 but were then fighting the Germans and the Italians in Egypt and in the Mediterranean, advocated a more indirect approach, one that featured strategic bombing, encouraging revolts among the subjugated peoples, and military actions on the periphery of the Axis-dominated world. They flatly rejected an American plan for an invasion of occupied France in the fall of 1942, code-named SLEDGEHAMMER, and argued for a combined Anglo-American invasion of French North Africa instead. President Roosevelt, who wanted U.S. forces fighting the Germans somewhere before the end of the year, forced his reluctant military leaders to agree.

This left the problem of what to tell the Soviets, who felt, with some reason, that they had been promised a second front in 1942. Churchill volunteered to go to Moscow—a long and dangerous journey by plane—and give the bad news to Stalin personally. The prime minister asked Roosevelt to send along W. Averell Harriman, who had served as the president's personal emissary to Churchill and to Stalin, in order to demonstrate Anglo-American solidarity. On August 12, 1942, they set out on the last leg of their journey in a B-24 Liberator bomber.

Since the roar of the engines made conversation impossible in the uninsulated aircraft interior, Churchill and Harriman passed notes back and forth. Some of these were frivolous, as when Churchill in mock exasperation gave mythical demerits to his bodyguard for failing to provide mustard for their ham-sandwich lunches. Other exchanges, including the one shown here, were more substantial. Knowing that Stalin would be disappointed, if not angered, by the cancellation of SLEDGEHAMMER, Harriman asked Churchill if there was any practical aid that the British could offer the hard-pressed Soviets. The prime minister replied that he would be willing, with Roosevelt's concurrence, to send British and American air squadrons once the Axis forces led by the brilliant general Erwin Rommel had been defeated. It is interesting to note that Churchill's reply both emphasized the limited air strength that the United Kingdom had to offer and envisioned an increase in the American air units fighting under British control in the Middle East.

In Moscow, Stalin reacted to Churchill's bad news about SLEDGEHAMMER by accusing the British and the Americans of cowardice. Churchill vigorously denied the accusation and offered to send air forces to southern Russia once Rommel had been crushed. He also told Stalin about the projected invasion of North Africa, now code-named TORCH. Inside the same noisy plane on the trip home, Harriman, who had not been present at the final meeting, scribbled a note asking Churchill for Stalin's reaction: "Did he agree to accept 'Torch' as the Second Front when it is started?" Churchill replied, "No but he thinks it absolutely right, & of great indirect advantage to Russia."

Churchill forwarded to Roosevelt his proposal (code-name VELVET)

Averell Harriman and Winston S. Churchill's handwritten notes written en route to Moscow, August 12, 1942, Library of Congress, Washington, D.C., Manuscript Division

I am particularly anxious to
know whether there are any
circumstances in which you will
offer Stalin during this visit air assistance on the
Southern Front with or without
U.S. participation.

When we have beaten Rommel we are willing
to offer about 17 Squadrons from U.S. & but these exclude some
U.S. squadrons now helping on. Without the 3 US Transport
Sqs. the Force cd not be maintained

Of course I cannot make a firm offer without
President's specific consent.
I shall therefore state this, & that I will ask
for it, if S. desires it; He may not

In addition I propose to President an effort
to raise this force to 30 or even 40 Squadrons.
The extra cd only be US. Squadron.
However the President has called me
saying he likes the idea & that he
does not think we ought to delay it till
after the battle in Egypt. This no doubt
applies to his additional American Squadrons
& not to those now working for us, or to our own

It will be necessary to clear this up by
cable, & also perhaps your own friend now
in Moscow may have news.

about sending a combined Anglo-American air force, operating under overall Soviet command, to the Caucasus mountains. The president was enthusiastic about the idea. After the Red Army inflicted heavy defeats upon the Germans around Stalingrad in November 1942, however, Stalin asked the Americans and British to send unmanned planes rather than complete air squadrons, and the proposal was eventually dropped.

[Transcript of handwritten notes between Averell Harriman and Winston S. Churchill, August 12, 1942]

[W. AVERELL HARRIMAN:]

I am particularly anxious to know whether there are any circumstances in which you will offer Stalin during this visit assistance on the Southern Front with or without U.S. participation.

[WINSTON S. CHURCHILL:]

When we have beaten Rommel we are willing to offer about 17 squadrons from ME but these include some US squadrons now helping us. Without the 3 US transport Sqns. the Force c[oul]d not be maintained. Of course I cannot make a firm offer without President's specific consent.

I shall therefore state this & that I will ask for it, if S[talin] desires it. He may not.

In addition I proposed to President an effort to raise this force to 30 or even 40 Squadrons. The extra c[oul]d only be US Squadrons.

However the President has cabled me saying he likes the idea & that he does not think we ought to delay it till after the battle in Egypt. This no doubt applies to his additional American Squadrons & not to those now working for us, or to our own.

It will be necessary to clear this up by cable, & also perhaps y[ou]r air general now in Moscow may have news.

D-Day and the "Bodyguard of Lies"

For the Americans helping to plan the course of World War II, an invasion of northwest Europe, to be undertaken as soon as possible, was to be the climax of the titanic struggle. For Winston Churchill, matters were not so simple. His experiences fighting Germans in World War I—when a generation of British men had been devastated by trench warfare and a series of costly and ill-advised frontal assaults—had predisposed him to seek other ways of defeating the Nazis. In 1940 and 1941, the armies of Britain and the Commonwealth nations had suffered an unbroken string of defeats at the hands of the Wehrmacht. In 1942 he had outlined his strategic ideas to a dubious Stalin: Germany, like a crocodile, should be attacked, not through the heavily armored "snout," but by knifing into the "soft belly" exposed along the Mediterranean shoreline and the Balkan Peninsula.

At first, his ideas governed the employment of the Anglo-American forces. After TORCH—the invasion of French North Africa—was successfully launched, Churchill managed to persuade Roosevelt and the American planners to follow up with further operations in the Mediterranean. Following the surrender of Axis troops in Tunisia in May 1943, the Allied armies catapulted into Sicily in July and then onto the Italian peninsula in September. As the war went on, other alternatives suggested themselves to him. One was a return to Norway, where the British had suffered a humiliating defeat in 1940. Such an operation would secure the northern sea route to the Soviet Union from attack. It would also provide a theater for employing one of his favorite ideas: a gigantic floating airfield (HABBAKUK) made out of a supposedly unsinkable, artificial iceberg. A second alternative was the seizure of the Dodecanese islands. This action would, Churchill felt, array the Turks actively on the side of the Allies.

At the August 1943 Quebec Conference, however, Churchill reaffirmed the British commitment to the cross-Channel invasion (OVERLORD), now scheduled for the spring of 1944. He did so with some misgivings. Casualties from such a direct assault might be catastrophically high. Men and equipment

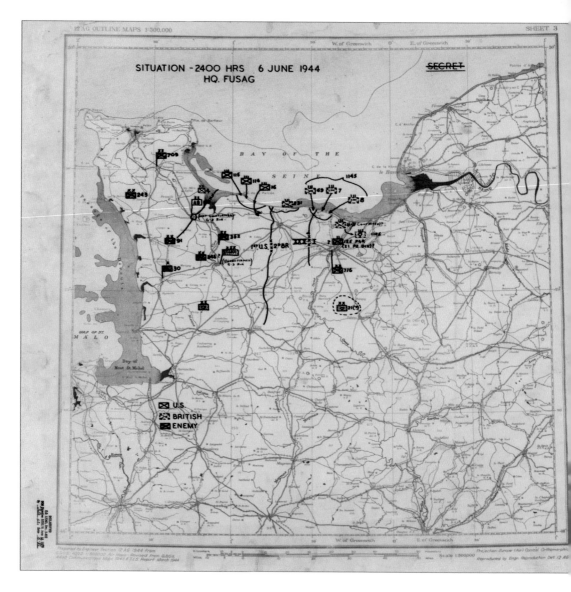

D-Day Situation Map, June 6, 1944, Library of Congress, Washington, D.C.,
Geography and Map Division. Detail shown on opposite page.

would have to be withdrawn from the Mediterranean, where things looked
promising and where British forces and British leadership predominated
(notwithstanding the overall command of the American general Dwight
David Eisenhower). Churchill feared that a lack of resources would prevent
the Allies from taking advantage of unforeseen opportunities for action, and
that British forces withdrawn to prepare for OVERLORD would be sitting idle
for many months. The American military chiefs viewed his alternatives as

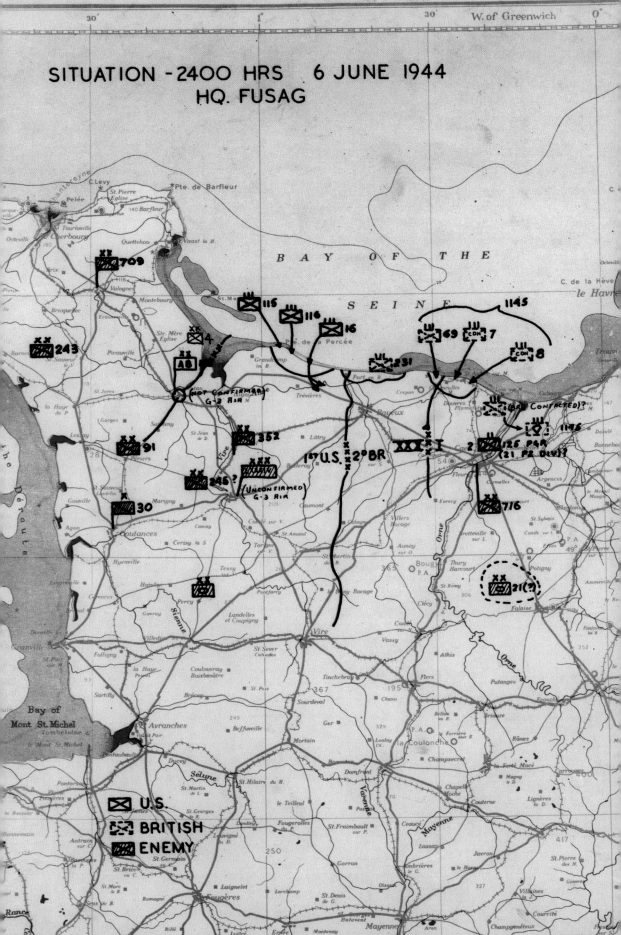

SITUATION - 2400 HRS   6 JUNE 1944
HQ. FUSAG

useless diversions. They also were suspicious of Churchill's motives, which they suspected came at least in part from a desire to preserve the British Empire after the war.

Stalin, playing tiebreaker at the Tehran Conference (November–December 1943), finally forced the issue. He accused Churchill of not backing OVERLORD, and he prodded the British and Americans to take a firm and final stand by naming a supreme commander. (Roosevelt selected Eisenhower, allowing overall command in the Mediterranean to pass into British hands.) The American and British military leaders at Tehran decided to launch the attack on the northern coast of France in May 1944; they also agreed to undertake a supporting operation on the southern (Mediterranean) French coast on as large a scale as possible. The decision having finally been made, Churchill tried to reassure Stalin about his commitment to a strong OVERLORD, a commitment that meant, in effect, no more diversions in the Balkans or eastern Mediterranean and a definite limitation on the amount of strength allotted to Allied forces in Italy. Churchill also called for a cover plan "to confuse and deceive the enemy as to the real time and place of our joint blows." "Truth," he said, "deserves a bodyguard of lies."

The great invasion was finally launched on D-Day, June 6, 1944. Refusing to be governed by his fears, Churchill had worked energetically for OVERLORD's success. By the time of the actual invasion he had become enthusiastic enough to try to participate personally—ostensibly as an observer on board a British warship that was to bombard the German coast defenses. When General Eisenhower objected, he said that the supreme commander had no right to dictate the composition of His Majesty's forces, and in his capacity as defense minister he had the power simply to assign himself to some British unit for the landings. It took the personal intervention of King George VI to overrule this plan, thus effectively ending Churchill's dream of seeing combat once again at the age of sixty-nine. Six days later, however, he did visit the beachhead and, while returning across the Channel, had the destroyer in which he was sailing open fire on enemy targets.

The landings and subsequent build-up were successful, thanks in part to the cover/deception plan that Churchill had mentioned at Tehran. The most important object was to convince the Germans that the landings in Normandy were only a feint, and that the main assault was to come ashore at the Pas de Calais, the point at which Britain is closest to the Continent. A largely non-existent, troopless unit was established—the First United States Army Group (FUSAG)—with the famous American general George S. Patton, Jr., as its commander. For the sake of verisimilitude, wireless operators dispatched a flood of meaningless, coded messages from the mythical headquarters and its subordinate units. Also, as this FUSAG Headquarters map shows, documents with the appropriate (i.e., misleading) headings were created to fool any Germans into whose hands they might fall into thinking that Patton's army group really existed as a fighting force.

The secret situation map reproduced here, showing troop dispositions as of midnight on the sixth of June, is accurate enough to be convincing. Omaha Beach, not labeled, is just to the east of Pointe de la Percée. Here the 116th Infantry, a regiment of the Twenty-ninth Infantry Division attached to the First Infantry Division for the assault, suffered high casualties but succeeded in establishing its part of the beachhead. It should also be noted that some Allied units are missing from this depiction. Most notable among these is the Eighty-second Airborne Division, which had been airdropped with the 101st Airborne around Sainte Mère Église, to the north of Carentan.

Winston Churchill—American

Many Americans had known of Winston Churchill long before his, and Britain's, finest hour. Those who followed European politics knew him as the almost impossibly talented son of a famous father. They had watched with interest his transition from aristocratic conservative, to reforming liberal, and then back again to the Tory Party and his father's old post of chancellor of the exchequer. The reading public in the United States was well aware of his prodigious literary output: first as a daring war correspondent, then as biographer of his father and of the first Duke of Marlborough (his illustrious ancestor), and finally as chronicler of the Great War of 1914–18, in which he had played so important a role. Churchill's lesser efforts—a multitude of newspaper and magazine articles—had also attracted a wide American audience. His delightful and engaging memoir *A Roving Commission: My Early Life* had been published in the United States to great acclaim in 1930, when it seemed as though his political career had ended.

It was during World War II, however, that Churchill won the hearts and captured the imaginations of Americans. His inspirational speeches were widely rebroadcast throughout North America. In movie theaters all across the United States, newsreels showed Churchill leading his nation against the Axis enemy—at first alone, then together with his American and Soviet allies. Flashing his trademark V-for-Victory sign and puffing his ever-present cigar, he became an American icon.

Throughout the postwar years, Americans continued to cherish the memory of his wartime leadership. Presidents Harry S. Truman and Dwight D. Eisenhower had been colleagues during World War II, whose story Churchill, an author once more, had recounted in six best-selling volumes. The two presidents had continued their amicable relationships with him during the Cold War and Churchill's 1951–55 term as prime minister. President John F. Kennedy, a much younger man, had first encountered Churchill when his father, Joseph P. Kennedy, had been the United States ambassador to the United Kingdom in the late 1930's and early 1940's. Unlike his father, the younger Kennedy had been an unabashed admirer. In the final year of his tragically curtailed tenure, he took the opportunity to do that which his predecessor, Eisenhower, had declined (on the advice of his chief legal and diplomatic subordinates). On April 9, 1963, Kennedy signed a congressionally authorized proclamation conferring honorary citizenship upon Churchill, a distinction accorded only once before in America's history (to the Revolutionary War hero the Marquis de Lafayette). In his remarks, which Churchill watched in England via live satellite broadcast, Kennedy said:

In the dark days and darker nights when England stood alone—and most men save Englishmen despaired of England's life—he mobilized the English language and sent it into battle. The incandescent quality of his words illuminated the courage of his countrymen. . . . By adding his name to our rolls, we mean to honor him—but his acceptance honors us far more. For no statement or proclamation can enrich his name now—the name Sir Winston Churchill is already legend.

This cartoon, drawn by Leslie Illingworth to commemorate the event for the London *Daily Mail*, dramatically illustrates the personal connection by which Churchill bridged the destinies of two great nations.

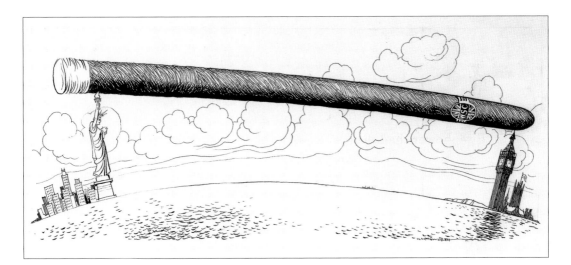

Leslie Illingworth's cartoon in the London *Daily Mail*, April 10, 1963,
Library of Congress, Washington, D.C., Prints and Photographs Division

American readers and researchers not able to have immediate access to the wealth of original documents held with the Churchill Papers and related collections at the Churchill Archives Centre, Churchill College, Cambridge, U.K., may nonetheless consider themselves fortunate enough to have available for consultation the eight-volume official biography *Winston S. Churchill*, by Randolph S. Churchill and Sir Martin Gilbert (Boston, Mass.: Houghton Mifflin, 1966–1988). These works are supplemented by Companion Volumes, including three volumes (to date) edited by Gilbert and published by W.W. Norton as *The Churchill War Papers* (1993–2001). The Companion Volumes reproduce the most important texts from a multitude of different sources. Collectively, Sir Martin's brilliant and monumental works constitute the starting point for all serious study of Winston Churchill.

    The items featured in this essay have come from the rich and vast collections of the Library of Congress. For "The Charge of the Twenty-first Lancers," Churchill's letter to his cousin is taken from the Marlborough Papers in the custody of the Library's Manuscript Division. The dust-jacket photograph described in "The Road to Fame" is in the Prints and Photographs Division. Other materials illustrating Churchill's adventures during the Boer War may be located in the Manuscript Division's Moreton Frewen and Reid Family holdings. Most of the letters cited in the "Teddy and Winnie" article may be found in the Theodore Roosevelt and Reid Family papers. These collections are also in the Manuscript Division. Other documents for this essay may be located in *The Letters of Theodore Roosevelt*, edited by Elting E. Morison *et al.* (8 vols; Cambridge, Mass.: Harvard University Press, 1951–4). The letter featured in "Redemption By Fire" comes from the Marlborough Papers; the quotation from Clementine Churchill describing the effect that the failure of the Dardanelles expedition had on her husband, along with other documents and information, may be found in Martin Gilbert, *Winston S. Churchill, Volume III, 1914–1916 The Challenge of War* (Boston, Mass.: Houghton Mifflin, 1971), and in its two Companion Volumes. The photograph used for the essay on "The Atlantic Conference," as well as the handwritten notes described in "VELVET and the Second Front" are taken from the Papers of Averell Harriman in the Library of Congress. The Library's Geography and Map Division holds the situation map used to illustrate "D-Day and the Bodyguard of Lies." (The quotation about the "soft belly" of the German "crocodile" is taken from "Minutes of a Meeting Held in the Kremlin, Moscow, on Thursday, August 13th, 1942, at 11.15 p.m."; the "bodyguard" quotation comes from the "Summary of the Third Regular Session of the Tehran Meeting," November 30, 1943, both in the Averell Harriman Papers.) Leslie Illingworth's original cartoon, which is featured in "Winston Churchill—American," may be found in the holdings of the Library's Prints and Photographs Division. The quotation from President Kennedy cited in that essay may be found in *Public Papers of the Presidents of the United States: John F. Kennedy, January 1 to November 22, 1963* (Washington, D.C.: U.S. Government Printing Office, 1964).

ABOUT THE LIBRARY OF CONGRESS

The Library of Congress, established in 1800, is America's oldest federal cultural institution. It is the largest repository of recorded knowledge in the world with more than 125 million items in more than 450 different languages. It simultaneously serves as Congress's working research collection, the national library, and a powerful symbol of the central role that free access to information plays in a knowledge-based democracy. The Library's mission is to make its resources available and useful to the Congress and the American people and to sustain and preserve a universal collection of knowledge and creativity for future generations. For more information about the Library of Congress visit http://www.loc.gov.

"Churchill and the Great Republic" draws on collections of the Library of Congress and the Churchill Archives Centre to explore Sir Winston Churchill's life and achievements. The exhibition includes nearly 200 items presenting a wide array of materials including documents, letters, speeches, photographs, prints, maps, audio-visual materials, and three-dimensional artifacts. An online version of the exhibition can be viewed at http://www.loc.gov/exhibits.

The Churchill Centre, co-publisher of this book in association with the Library of Congress, appreciates the valuable contributions made to it by The Lady Soames DBE, Sir Martin Gilbert and The Librarian of Congress, Dr. James H. Billington; and to Mr. Allen Packwood and Mr. Daun van Ee for superbly compiling, organizing and describing the documents that appear both in the exhibition and in this book.

We at The Churchill Centre, an international organization of nearly 3,000 members dedicated to teaching younger generations worldwide those universal traits and values essential to civilized society personified by Winston Churchill, welcome this opportunity to collaborate with the Library of Congress and the Churchill Archives at Churchill College in Cambridge, England, in both the preparation of this book and other activities related to the wonderful exhibit, "Churchill and the Great Republic."

For more information about The Churchill Centre, please visit our website, www.winstonchurchill.org; write us at 1150 17TH Street, NW, Suite 307, Washington, D.C. 20036; or call us toll free at (888) WSC-1874.

William C. Ives
President

ABOUT THE CHURCHILL ARCHIVES CENTRE

The Churchill Archives Centre, Cambridge U.K., was built in 1973 thanks largely to the generosity of distinguished American citizens. It is part of Churchill College, itself the British National and Commonwealth memorial to Sir Winston, and one of the constituent colleges of the University of Cambridge. In addition to the archive of Sir Winston Churchill, the Centre holds an additional 570-plus collections of private papers, documenting the history of the Churchill era and beyond. It collects the archives of prominent individuals working in the fields of politics, diplomacy, grand strategy and science: those areas of public life in which Churchill played a role or took a keen interest. The Centre houses many contemporary collections, including the papers of Baroness Thatcher.

The role of the Archives Centre is to preserve and to present this material so that it can be used for the benefit of research and education. For more information about the Churchill Archives Centre, please visit www.chu.cam.ac.uk/archives/.

The Churchill Papers were bought with the aid of the Heritage Lottery Fund in 1995, and are now administered by the Sir Winston Churchill Archive Trust. The Centre would also like to acknowledge the support of the Master, Fellows and Scholars of Churchill College, Cambridge, and the help of Winston S. Churchill and The Lady Soames, both Honorary Fellows of the College.

Colophon

This main text of this book has been set in the digital form of Monotype Walbaum
with the correspondence set in Adobe Garamond
and descriptive notes to the correspondence set in Gill Sans.

WALBAUM

The first cutting of Walbaum was made in the late eighteenth century
by Justus Erich Walbaum, whose first engravings were of pastry
molds while apprenticed to a confectioner. He later began cutting
music types and eventually set up his own foundry in the town of Goslar.
Walbaum is in the tradition of the Didot types,
but its particular eccentricities give it a warmth and character
quite different from the more severe, rational types
of Didot and Bodoni.

GARAMOND

Adobe's Garamond family, designed by Robert Slimbach,
is a digital interpretation of the roman types of Claude Garamond
and the italic types of Robert Granjon.
Garamond's types were based on the Venetian types of the fifteenth century
and have been among the most popular faces of the last four hundred years.
This contemporary Garamond carries the elegance of the
original and the practicality of a full font family
for digital bookmaking.

GILL SANS

is one of the most esteemed sans serif faces of the twentieth century.
It is based on the typeface designed for the London Underground by Edward Johnston;
Eric Gill, a student of Johnston, was an artist as well as a type designer,
and had earlier designed Perpetua for Stanley Morison, the designer of Times New Roman.
Gill Sans is known as a humanist sans serif, and its departures from the pure,
geometric sans serifs are part of its appeal, along with a flared capital R
which finds a continental cousin in Walbaum,
and an eyeglass lowercase g, a character Baskerville
might well have appreciated.

First published in 2004 by GILES
an imprint of D Giles Limited
57 Abingdon Road, London, W8 6AN, U.K.
www.gilesltd.com

ISBN: 1 904832 00 8

FOR THE LIBRARY OF CONGRESS:
Director of Publishing: W. Ralph Eubanks
Director of Interpretive Programs: Irene U. Chambers
Editorial Assistant: Aimee Hess
Copy Editor: Ellen Coughlin

Designed by Michael Hentges Design, Alexandria, Virginia
Produced by GILES, an imprint of D Giles Limited
Printed and bound in Italy by Sfera International srl, Milan
Photographs are by Lee Anderson, Library of Congress, and Mark Scudder

LIBRARY OF CONGRESS CATALOGING-IN-PUBLICATION DATA

Gilbert, Martin, 1936-
    Churchill and the great republic / preface by Mary Churchill Soames; foreword by James H.
Billington; essays by Martin Gilbert, Daun van Ee, and Allen Packwood.
    p. cm.
    Accompanies the exhibition, Churchill and the Great Republic, held at the Library of Congress,
Washington, D.C. in 2004.
    ISBN 1 904832 00 8 (alk. paper)
    1. Churchill, Winston, Sir, 1874–1965—Exhibitions. 2. Great Britain—Politics and government—20th
century—Exhibitions. 3. Great Britain—Foreign relations—United States—Exhibitions. 4. United
States—Foreign relations—Great Britain—Exhibitions. 5. Prime ministers—Great Britain—
Biography—Exhibitions. I. Van Ee, Daun, 1946– . II. Packwood, Allen. III. Library of Congress.
IV. Title.
DA566.9.C5 G445 2004
941.084'092—DC22
    2003023897